Uruguay

Uruguay

BY MARION MORRISON

Enchantment of the World
Second Series

Children's Press®

A Division of Scholastic Inc.

NEW YORK   TORONTO   LONDON   AUCKLAND   SYDNEY
MEXICO CITY   NEW DELHI   HONG KONG
DANBURY, CONNECTICUT

Frontispiece: Horseman and cattle in the Cuchilla Grande

Consultant: Carmen Madariaga Culver, Academic Director, Latin American Southern Cone
Programs, State University of New York–Plattsburgh

Please note: All statistics are as up-to-date as possible at the time of publication.

Book production by Herman Adler Design

Library of Congress Cataloging-in-Publication Data

Morrison, Marion.
  Uruguay / by Marion Morrison.
        p. cm. — (Enchantment of the World. Second series)
  Includes bibliographical references and index.
  ISBN 0-516-23682-2
    1. Uruguay—Juvenile literature. I. Title. II. Series.
    F2708.5.M673 2005
    989.5—dc22   2004019420

Uruguay

Contents

Cover photo:
Uruguayan
gaucho

CHAPTER

 **ONE** Welcome to Uruguay 8

TWO Land of Grasslands, Rivers, and Lakes 16

THREE Wetlands and Wildlife 30

FOUR The Banda Oriental 44

FIVE Governing the Country 62

SIX An Agricultural Economy 72

SEVEN People of Uruguay 84

EIGHT Freedom of Faiths 94

NINE Culture, Arts, and Sports 102

TEN Daily Life 118

Saint Teresa
National Park

Timeline.....................**128**

Fast Facts...................**130**

To Find Out More **134**

Index **136**

Comparsas dancer

Welcome to Uruguay

I F YOU LOVE OLD CARS, THEN URUGUAY IS THE PLACE TO GO. The tiny republic in South America, wedged between the giant countries of Argentina and Brazil, is a treasure chest of old cars. The cars are known as *cachilas*, and you will find them in Montevideo, the capital city, and in small towns and villages. Some are kept on the streets, occasionally with a big "For Sale" sign attached; others are in the backyards of houses, and still more are garaged. Most date back more than fifty years. The many models include Fords—even Model Ts—Buicks, Chevrolets, Studebakers, and British cars such as Jaguars, Hillmans, and even Daimlers similar to the one used by Queen Elizabeth II. The cachilas have been lovingly maintained and restored over the years, with the parts of one often used to repair another. Sometimes this results in a curious sort of hybrid model. But the important thing is that the old cars still work. They are still used to carry people and produce, and a few tradespeople still use them as delivery vans. In recent years foreigners have shown an interest in buying the cachilas, but the Uruguayan government has placed restrictions on their export. So why are there so many old cars? The answer lies in the first half of the twentieth century, a time when a prosperous Uruguay was known as "the new Switzerland."

Let's go back even further in history for a moment. Like most other countries in South America, Uruguay became a Spanish colony after the Europeans arrived at the beginning

Opposite: **Well-cared-for cachilas can be found throughout Uruguay.**

Cattle farming began when the Spaniards introduced cattle to Uruguay.

of the sixteenth century. Some three hundred years later, in 1828, it became an independent republic. The Spaniards had introduced cattle and sheep into the tiny colony, and the animals thrived on the hilly grasslands. The herds continued to grow, and an industry developed in meat, leather, and wool. After gaining its independence, Uruguay had many troubled years as military men and political leaders vied for power. Then, toward the end of the nineteenth century, things began to change. Tens of thousands of immigrants, mainly from Europe, arrived and settled, bringing with them new ideas and technologies. A period of relative peace led to the creation of modern Uruguay, with immigrants making up much of the new middle and working classes.

In the early years of the twentieth century, another period of political unrest was brought to an end by Uruguay's perhaps most respected president, José Batlle y Ordóñez (1903–1907 and 1911–1915). He did more than bring peace; he also introduced into Uruguay social reforms that were very advanced for the time. The reforms included ensuring proper working conditions for the people and state aid for people who were unemployed, sick, or elderly. These were good years for Uruguay. The population of mainly European immigrants and their descendants had a democratically elected government, a thriving economy, and a welfare state that was among the best in the world.

World Wars I and II brought more prosperity. By this time Uruguay had another secret weapon. In 1865, Justus von Liebig, an enterprising German, had developed a company that manufactured meat extract in a small town, Fray Bentos, on the Río (River) Uruguay. Forty years later thousands of people were employed in factories producing the extract and canned meat. Both were highly valued products in great demand during the wars. The prosperity of those years allowed Uruguayans to acquire luxuries and live well. In the Switzerland of the Americas, cars were one of those luxuries.

After World War II ended in 1945, the economy went into decline. The meat factories closed, and the original plant was restored as a museum, Museo de la Revolución Industrial

During the late 1800s, the town of Fray Bentos prospered as a result of its meat-extracting factories.

(Museum of the Industrial Revolution). Political turmoil along with several years of terrorism, and finally a military coup followed. The country returned to democratic rule and a stable government in the mid-1980s. People have hung on to the old cars for both nostalgic and economic reasons.

The Capital

The heart of Uruguay is its capital city, Montevideo. Founded in 1726, it stands on the northern shore of the Río de la Plata (River of Silver or River Plate) estuary and has one of the finest harbors in the region. The historic part of the city lies within just a few blocks of the port. Plaza de la Constitución, also known as Plaza Matriz, is the oldest square in

Since the early days of Montevideo, its oldest square, Plaza de la Constitución, has played an important role in daily life.

Montevideo. Catedral Matriz (Metropolitan Cathedral), built between 1790 and 1804, stands on one side of the square, and on the other stands *el Cabildo*, the old town hall, built in 1804, where the independence of Uruguay was plotted and planned. A statue of the founder of the city, Bruno Mauricio de Zabala can also be found in Montevideo. The old city of Montevideo has grown and now includes residential and industrial suburbs, shopping areas, a financial center, many parks, and miles of beautiful beaches. Few other cities in the world so dominate their country as Montevideo does Uruguay. Nearly 4 million people live in Uruguay, and more than a third of them are in Montevideo. It is the country's cultural, financial, and industrial center and its most important port.

Outside the city the endless miles of grasslands, dotted with a few hills, seem empty. There are some small towns and a few villages bordering the Río Uruguay and other rivers along the south coast. There also are areas devoted to agriculture. But much of the interior is empty except for cattle and sheep. Here and there are *estancias*, or ranches, some very large, others quite small, where gauchos, or cowboys, live and work. Centuries

A statue honors Montevideo's founding father, Bruno Mauricio de Zabala.

Cattle graze on the grasslands of Uruguay.

This painting from 1820 celebrates the gaucho.

ago gauchos spent the days out on the plains, moving great herds to new pastures and sleeping under the stars. In times of war, they proved to be brave and fearless fighters. Today their history is very much part of the country's folklore. At rodeos and other fiestas they still demonstrate their horsemanship. They have been painted by artists and glorified in literature, perhaps nowhere more so than in the epic poem

URUGUAY
- Cities of over 40,000 people
- Other cities
- National capital

0 ____ 80 miles
0 ____ 80 kilometers

Bella Unión
Artigas
Río Cuareim
Tomás Gomensoro
Lake Salto Grande
Belén
Rivera
Constitucion
Tranqueras
Salto

ARGENTINA

Corrales
Tacuarembó

Paysandú
Guichón
San Gregorio
Río Negro
Fraile Muerto
Melo
Laguna Merín

BRAZIL

Young
Nuevo Berlin
Lake Palmar
Embalse Rincón del Bonete
Santa Clara
Vergara
Río Branco
Fray Bentos
Mercedes
Carmen
Cerro Chato
Treinta y Tres
Frontier
Durazno
Río Yi
Sarandí del Yi
Dolores
Trinidad
Sarandí Grande
José Pedro Varela
Aiguá
Chuy
Nueva Palmira
Cardona
Casupá
Carmelo
Suárez
Rosario
San Ramón
Florida
Tala
Aiguá
Castillos
Colonia del Sacramento
Juan Lacaze
Canelones
Pando
Minas
Rocha
Las Piedras
Pan de Azúcar
La Paloma
Río de la Plata
Montevideo
Piriápolis
Maldonado
Punta del Este

ATLANTIC OCEAN

Río Uruguay

N W E S

"The Gaucho Martín Fierro," written by the Argentinian José
Hernández in 1872:

A son am I of the rolling plain
A gaucho born and bred
And this is my pride; to live as free
As the bird that cleaves the sky.

Land of Grasslands, Rivers, and Lakes

U RUGUAY IS THE SECOND SMALLEST SOUTH AMERICAN country. Only Suriname is smaller. Uruguay is almost the same size as Washington State. To the north and northeast it shares a 612-mile (985-kilometer) border with the giant country of Brazil. To the west the Río Uruguay forms the border with Argentina, along with the broad estuary of the Río de la Plata along the southwest. The east coast of Uruguay faces the Atlantic Ocean. Montevideo, the capital, stands on the north shore of the Río de la Plata estuary, which is also the southern shore of Uruguay. Uruguay has two large expanses of fresh water. One is the largest artificial lake in South America, Embalse Rincón de Bonete, and the other is a major coastal lagoon, Laguna Merín, which it shares with Brazil. Combined with smaller expanses of fresh water, they account for 1.5 percent of the total area of the country.

Opposite: **Though a small country, Uruguay's landscape varies from rolling countryside to plains and coastline.**

The Landscape

Much of Uruguay sits on a base of ancient crystalline rock and granite. In the north and central parts the base is overlaid with horizontal layers of rock dating back as much as 286 million years. The plains in the southwest are composed primarily of geologically recent sediments and deposits carried by the great rivers. In some places rocks protrude to form ridges or rows of hills known locally as *cuchillas*. None are very high, and they lend a rolling aspect to the otherwise even land-

Uruguay's Geographical Features

Area: 68,039 square miles (176,220 sq km)

Largest city: Montevideo, population 1,346,900

Highest Elevation: Cerro Catedral, 1,683 feet (513 m)

Lowest Elevation: sea level at coast

Highest Temperature Recorded: 107°F (42°C)

Lowest Temperature Recorded: 39°F (4°C)

Longest River: Río Negro, approximately 500 miles (800 km)

Largest Lake (artificial): Embalse Rincón del Bonete

Largest Lagoon (shared with Brazil): Laguna Merín

Coastline: 410 miles (660 km)

scape. Two of the cuchillas are large. The Cuchilla de Haedo in the north stretches from the Brazilian border southward for about 125 miles (201 km). The small departmental capital of Tacuarembó lies in its eastern foothills. The Cuchilla Grande crosses from the east of the country almost to the Atlantic coast in the south in the department of Maldonado. It is here in the south that the highest elevations in the country are found. Cerro Catedral is 1,683 feet (513 meters) high. The

Mirador Nacional, which is 1,644 feet (501 m) high, is sometimes known as the Cerro de las Ánimas, or Hill of Souls, from a legend of the Charrúa people who once populated the land.

From these lookouts a grass-covered, gently rolling land reaches as far as the eye can see. Here and there pockets of trees nestle in shallow valleys, and in early summer wildflowers fleck the roadside with brilliant color. The country is seldom dry, and streams and small rivers fill numerous shallow gullies, or arroyos. Dry gullies fill with water after it rains.

The land to the west drains into the Río Uruguay and eventually into the Río de la Plata estuary. In the center and the north the flow is to the Río Negro, which is the largest of the country's rivers. The Río Negro ultimately flows into the Río Uruguay. Drainage to the east is either directly into the Atlantic or into coastal lagoons such as Laguna Merín. A few small arroyos flow directly into the Río de la Plata estuary.

The Cuchilla Grande is a range of hills found in eastern Uruguay.

Colorful Crystals

One of the wonders from the ancient geological past is the wealth of minerals found in Uruguay. The city of Artigas in the north is famous for agate and amethyst found in the Arapey Formation, a geological structure about 130 million years old. In the upper reaches of an arroyo called Catalán Grande, simple mining uncovers many geodes, which are rocks with a cavity. These geodes hold amethyst crystals of an intense violet. Most of the geodes are small, no more than a few inches across. For larger specimens the collector has to look to other arroyos where some of these magnificent rocks are more than 3 feet (1 m) from end to end. The stones are sold as specimens in their geodes or are cut and polished for jewelry.

The Río Uruguay

The Río Uruguay is one of South America's major rivers. It has a total length of 990 miles (1,593 km), of which 360 miles (579 km) are in Uruguay. The river rises in southeastern Brazil in a range of low mountains close to the Atlantic coast. Another Brazilian river, the Pelotas, joins the Río Uruguay. The river continues with the name Pelotas until, while still in Brazil, it becomes the Uruguay. The river gathers more water from many tributaries, and in extreme wet seasons it attains a flow of 1,060,000 cubic feet (30,016 cubic meters) per second. The annual average flow is less impressive,

The Río Uruguay forms the entire border with Argentina.

with fluctuations between 158,000 and 175,000 cubic feet (4,474 and 4,955 cu m) per second. This is about twice the flow of Niagara Falls.

The huge river reaches Uruguay in the far northwest of the country at Bella Unión, where the Río Cuareim, a tributary, joins it from the east. The Río Cuareim flows from arroyos on the low Cuchilla Negra and forms part of the northern border. From Bella Unión the Uruguay flows almost due south, forming the border with Argentina.

Four major tributaries flow in from the slopes of the cuchillas. The first is the Río Arapey Grande, which begins in the Cuchilla de Haedo and enters the Río Uruguay between the towns of Belén and Constitución. These towns now stand at the edge of a lake created by a major dam at Salto Grande. Hot springs, or *termas*, are a feature of the land bordering the river and are a sign of the interactivity between the water and underlying rocks still warm from early geological activity. The Termas de Arapey contain water at 104 degrees Fahrenheit (40 degrees Celsius) flowing from a depth of more than 4,200 feet (1,280 m).

It was at Salto Grande, which means "Big Leap" or "Big Rapids," that the Río Uruguay was once broken by major rapids as the river flowed across exposed rock. The place was ideal for building a dam, and in 1982 the Salto Grande project, a hydroelectric plant, was completed. It was funded jointly by Argentina and Uruguay

The Salto hydroelectric dam produces power for Uruguay as well as Argentina.

to produce hydroelectric power for both countries. Salto is the nearest Uruguayan city, and from this point downstream the river is studded with rocks and small rapids, so it is difficult to navigate.

The Río Daymán, also from the Cuchilla de Haedo, enters just below Salto. The Termas de Daymán, with water reaching temperatures of 115°F (46°C), is nearby. The *meseta*, or plateau, of Artigas is the site of a national monument that stands 148 feet (45 m) above the river. Here the course narrows with more rocks over which the water flows briskly, forming whirlpools. The section is known as El Hervidero, or "The Boiling." More termas occur at the town of Guaviyú

Bathers enjoy the warm waters of the Termas de Guaviyú.

beside the small Arroyo Guaviyú that flows directly into the Río Uruguay.

The next major tributary entering downstream is the 175-mile (280-km) Río Queguay Grande, which begins as a small arroyo in hills near the town of Tambores in the Cuchilla de Haedo. In its middle course the Queguay Grande is joined by another river, the Queguay Chico, in a place known as the Rincón de los Gauchos. There is an abundance of trees and bushes along the edge of the rivers.

Just before the Queguay Grande reaches the Uruguay it passes over a band of hard rock in a 30-foot (9-m) waterfall known as the Cascades of Queguay. The outlet is just upstream from the small river port of Paysandú that is thought to be the farthest point on the Río Uruguay that oceangoing vessels can navigate.

A short distance above Paysandú, the General Artigas International Bridge crosses the river to Colón on the Argentinian side, and roads handle trade between the docks of the two countries. Below Paysandú the Río Uruguay is studded with islands and extends to as much as 5 miles (8 km) wide. Fray Bentos, with its once-important meat-extracting plant, is next with another major bridge crossing. Then at the small town of Soriano, the Río Negro enters through a delta with numerous very low and flat islands. Amid the narrow, tree-lined waterways is an island known as Vizcaíno, or the Biscayan, after people from Biscay in France. Established by missionaries in 1624, it was home to the first European settlement in Uruguay.

Floods

The huge rivers of Uruguay have a history of flooding. In 1959, the water levels of the Río Uruguay rose disastrously. The dam at Salto Grande had not yet been built, and water simply poured from the Brazilian headwaters. More recently rainfall has been aggravated by El Niño, a climatic phenomenon affecting many parts of the earth. In April 1998, eight thousand people were evacuated from towns in the north along the Río Uruguay and from the town of Treinta y Tres. Rice production in low areas by the Río Olimar and the Río Cebolatti was badly affected. In June 2001, the waters rose again, and the United Nations office in Montevideo reported that five thousand people had been evacuated, including 2,059 children.

Approximately 1,200 houses had been damaged, of which 240 were destroyed. In the same flood season the Río Cuareim reached a record level of 46.5 feet (14.2 m). Floods occurred again in October 2003 but not on the same scale.

The Río Negro

The Río Negro, the fourth major tributary of the Río Uruguay, is the longest river within the country. The source is in southern Brazil, not far from the city of Bagé. As the river flows into Uruguay, it follows a shallow depression from northeast to southwest between the two largest cuchillas. The flow of the river has been changed dramatically midcourse by three major dams that hold back the water in a series of lakes. One of these, the Embalse Rincón del Bonete, is the largest artificial lake in South America. A smaller lake just downstream is the feeder for a hydroelectric power station at Baygorria.

The Río Negro is about 500 miles long, the longest river in Uruguay.

Many smaller streams flow into the lake on all sides, and the entire region is the most productive in the country due to the water and plentiful electric power. Another large river, the Tacuarembó, drains into the northeastern corner of Embalse Rincón del Bonete, and the Río Yi flows into the new Lake Palmar at the southern end of the system. Another hydroelectric power station, at the new Palmar Constitución dam near Mercedes, is the last before the Río Negro resumes its true course to its delta.

Below the Río Negro delta the Río Uruguay broadens to up to 7.5 miles (12 km) wide until the width is restricted slightly by islands and sediments of the delta of the Río Paraná in Argentina. The flow from the Río Paraná dwarfs that of the Río Uruguay, but side by side they enter the huge estuary known as the Río de la Plata.

The Río de la Plata is a huge estuary lying between the south coast of Uruguay and the north coast of Argentina.

Río de la Plata

The Río de la Plata covers an area of approximately 13,500 square miles (34,965 sq km) and is bounded by Argentina to the south and a low-lying coastline, and by Uruguay to the north. At the narrowest point it is 31 miles (50 km) wide, and at its widest it is about 136 miles (219 km) across.

This estuary ranks among the giants. It empties into the Atlantic about 777,000 cubic feet (22,002 cu m) of fresh water per second. The Río Paraná, its tributaries, and the Río Uruguay drain about one-quarter of the area of South America. The Río de la Plata is tidal, and the effect reaches as far as 121 miles (195 km) up the rivers.

The Coast

Santa Teresa National Park is one area of Uruguay with a sandy coastline.

Uruguay has 136.6 miles (220 km) of Atlantic coastline. There are many sandy beaches, areas of dunes, and a low plain extending inland for up to 5 miles (8 km). An onshore wind drives the sand and some of the dunes such as those at Cabo Polonia as much as 98 feet (30 m) high. Rocky *puntas*, or points, jut into the sea in several places and have a history of causing shipwrecks.

This coast is known for its lagoons. Some are connected to the sea by a channel, and others are totally landlocked. They were created by the Atlantic Ocean's throwing up sand and sediment to form low-lying bars that are nonetheless higher than the land behind. Lagoons form in these depressions as fresh water flows mostly from arroyos. In places, the land around the lagoons is marshy and has been left as a natural habitat. In others it is used for growing rice. The largest lagoon, Laguna Merín, is shared with Brazil. Its total area is

1,542 square miles (3,994 sq km). Fresh water drains into this lagoon from numerous arroyos and rivers with headwaters in the Cuchilla Grande.

The Río Olimar Grande and the Río Cebolatti, which are Uruguayan, and the Río Yaguarón, which rises in Brazil, form a natural border. The Laguna Merín drains into a much larger lagoon to the north in Brazil known as the Lagoa dos Patos. South of the Laguna Merín and surrounded by marshland, the Laguna Negra is the largest that is totally in Uruguay. Others range along the coast to the Laguna de Sauce between the towns of Maldonado and Piriápolis.

Climate

The annual average temperature in Montevideo is 61°F (16°C). The hottest months are December, January, and February, when the temperature averages 81°F (27°C). The coolest months are June, July, and August, when the temperature averages 43°F (6°C). Inland, the temperatures tend to be several degrees warmer. In Salto the warmest three months average 86°F (30°C), and the coolest average 48°F (9°C).

Rainfall is lower in Montevideo than it is inland, with an annual total of 37.4 inches (95 centimeters), while in Salto the average annual total is 50.3 inches (128 cm). The country experiences sudden changes in temperature when a wind known as the pampero blows in from the pampas, or prairies, in the far southwest of the continent. The changing weather is often accompanied by days of rain and then finally by very clear, bright skies.

Looking at Uruguay's Cities

Colonia del Sacramento (below) is a small, historic town at the edge of the Río de la Plata. It is the capital of the department of the same name. The town was founded in 1680 by Manuel Lobo, the Portuguese governor of Rio de Janeiro, in what is now Brazil. For some years Colonia del Sacramento was at the heart of the rivalry between the Spanish and Portuguese South American territories. Today the town is a mixture of old and new with a population of approximately 22,200. Since 1968, there has been steady progress on the restoration of buildings dating from the colonial era, and the town has been granted World Heritage status by the United Nations Educational, Scientific, and Cultural Organization (UNESCO).

Treinta y Tres is a city of more than 27,500 people and the capital of the department of the same name. It stands on the northern bank of the Río Olimar 43 miles (70 km) west of Laguna Merín and 179 miles (286 km) by road from Montevideo. The name comes from the famous thirty-three (treinta y tres in Spanish) patriots led by General Juan Antonio Lavalleja, who crossed the Río Uruguay from Argentina in 1825 to liberate the Banda Oriental, as Uruguay was then known. The central square is named Plaza 19th Abril to commemorate

the day of the landing (April 19). The departmental emblem incorporates many historical symbols, including thirty-three lances. The department can also boast that it produces more than 50 percent of the country's rice. The local choir, the Coro Pro-Musica de Treinta y Tres, is known throughout Uruguay and has performed in the United States.

Salto (above) stands beside the Río Uruguay and was given its name after the nearby *salto*, meaning "leap" or "rapids." It is the capital of the department of the same name and the second largest city in Uruguay. The first settlement was established in the eighteenth century, but the economy only began to grow with the development of two private commercial banks in the nineteenth century. Later Uruguay and Argentina decided to develop a dam there between the two countries. In 1979, the first generator began to produce power, and by 1983, the project was fully operational. For small river craft a canal with locks was built, and the future of the city's economy was assured. The dam is 12 miles (20 km) north of Salto on the Río Uruguay and today is a major tourist attraction. The population is approximately 103,800.

Wetlands and Wildlife

WHEN THE FIRST SETTLERS ARRIVED, MUCH OF THE LAND to the east of the Río Uruguay was covered with grass, just as it is today. The vegetation is composed of numerous species of grass. Some of the plants are small and resemble prairie grasses; others are taller, and some, such as the elegant pampas grass, are often seen in parks and gardens in other parts of the world. Trees native to the area are confined to the hollows and the watercourses, where they are known as gallery forest. The mix of plants changes from region to region and within the few variations of altitude. The entire region is important environmentally because it represents a corridor between the flatlands of eastern Argentina and the southern parts of the extraordinarily diverse Atlantic coast rain forest of Brazil.

While the grassland may be the dominant feature in Uruguay, there are some remarkable special habitats. The numerous lagoons of the coastal region are bounded

Opposite: **Rheas inhabit Uruguay's widespread grasslands.**

Pampas grass can grow to a height of 13 feet.

by swamps and favored by migrating birds. To the immediate east of the Río Uruguay, several palm savannas, grasslands packed with hundreds of tall yataí palms, provide a refuge for birds. One of the largest of these areas is the Palmares of Guaviyú, close to the city of Paysandú. The Río Uruguay and the Río de la Plata are known for many species of fish and a river dolphin, while other mammals and birds live in secluded places along the banks. There are numerous amphibians, small lizards, and twenty-two species of snake, including four that are venomous. One is the regional variety of rattlesnake. A

Migrating birds are attracted to Uruguay's coastal wetlands.

small island offshore in the Atlantic and within sight of Punta del Este is home to a large seal colony.

Isla de Lobos, off Uruguay's southern coast, is home to seals.

Since the beginning of Uruguay's agricultural development, the native animals have been pushed back into the tiny pockets of remaining undeveloped habitat. Some species, such as the ocelot, a member of the cat family, have virtually disappeared; no sightings have been reported for a long time. Others have gone altogether. Some species, such as the rhea, a flightless bird resembling an ostrich, appear to have adapted to the intrusion.

Wetlands

Conservation of wildlife and the environment has had a slow start in Uruguay. There are few reserves or protected zones, and those that do exist are at an early stage of development. In 2000, a National System of Protected Rural Areas was established by law.

The National Flower

The national flower, the ceibo (*Erythrina crista-galli*), or common coral tree, is highly visible in parks and streets during its flowering season of November to February. The tree grows to about 8 feet (2.4 m) and belongs to the same family as peas and beans. Its scientific name is derived from *erythros*, a Greek word meaning red. The ceibo was adopted as the national flower by decree in December 1942.

In the modern world, where artificial drainage is used to increase the area of land available for farming, natural wetlands are becoming a rarity. Even more environmental pressure has been put on the plants and the animals, with the result that biodiversity is being reduced everywhere. In 1971, the International Conference on the Conservation of Wetlands and Waterfowl was held in Ramsar, a small city on the southern shore of the Caspian Sea in Iran. Representatives from many nations attended, and the result was the first major international agreement to consider problems facing the environment. The countries met periodically to identify important wetlands for conservation. These areas were known as Ramsar sites. In 1984, the conference selected the immense marshy area between the border with Brazil, Cabo Polonia, and southeast of Treinta y Tres for protection. The site includes the Uruguayan area of Laguna Merín, Laguna Negra, Laguna Castillos, and sections of the Río

Olimar and the Río Cebolatti. This Ramsar site covers over 1 million acres (over 404,685 hectares).

Birds

The wetlands are an important stopping place for at least nineteen species of migratory shorebirds that breed in the north of the Americas and spend their summers in Uruguay. Small flamingos such the Chilean flamingo are visitors from the southern region of South America, while many ducks, ibis, plovers, and lapwings frequent the edges of the lagoons.

Chilean flamingos take a rest in Uruguay on their trip north from southern areas in South America.

Almost all the 104 aquatic bird species recorded in Uruguay can be found in the wetlands. Among the notable

Black-necked swans make their home in the marshlands of Uruguay.

larger birds found there are the black-necked swan, the coscoroba swan, and the southern screamer, a bird with the body size of a goose but longer legs. Locally, southern screamers are known as *chajá*, and they are easily recognized by their two-note, trumpeting call.

The National Bird

The national bird is known affectionately as the *hornero*. It is the rufous hornero (*Furnarius rufus*), and it gets its name from its exquisitely made mud nest, which resembles the domed clay ovens once used by country people. Horneros seem to be unafraid of people. They are part of the regional folklore, as the early inhabitants felt that seeing one of the birds around the home was a good sign. These birds have a warm-brown upper plumage and lighter breast feathers. They feed on insects, worms, and larvae.

Mammals

There are far fewer mammal species than bird species in the wetlands. Among rodents, the capybara is common. Capybara, which reach the size of small pigs, or about 77–143 pounds (35–65 kilograms), are the largest rodents in the world. They are often seen in groups, particularly where the aquatic vegetation is dense. Another rodent of the marshlands is the coypu, which grows to about 1.64 feet (0.5 m), excluding

Below left: **Capybara are the largest rodents in the world. This is a mother capybara and her young.**

Below right: **Another rodent found in Uruguay is the semiaquatic coypu.**

In the wild, pampas deer have become threatened in Uruguay.

the scaly, ratlike tail. Coypu are mostly nocturnal and semiaquatic, inhabiting places with plenty of aquatic plants. They like the cover of bushes close to the arroyos, where they burrow in banks.

Otters, semiaquatic carnivores that feed on fish, and freshwater crustaceans such as shrimps are becoming endangered in much of South America. The otter of the wetlands, the neotropical otter, or *lobito del río*, can usually be detected by deposits of its feces. One of the rarest animals in the area is the pampas deer, which stands about 2.5 feet (0.8 m) at the shoulder. It is the only species of deer that exists in the wild in Uruguay. This fine animal has been under attack from hunters throughout its range in southern South America for many years, but fortunately it is surviving in the reserve.

Quebrada de los Cuervos Reserve

Quebrada means "ravine," which is the rugged path of a stream, and *cuervo* literally means "crow," though here the name is used for a vulture. The crow in the quebrada is the red-headed or turkey vulture (right), which has a wingspan of approximately 6 feet (1.8 m). These vultures feed largely on dead animals and can detect the smell of a carcass from quite a distance. Another bird that is typical of the reserve is the red-legged seriema, which is known throughout the drier parts of central-southern South America. These birds with long slender legs stand about 35 inches (0.9 m) high and feed on a variety of foods, including venomous snakes. Legend suggests that the birds are immune to the poison, though this is not true. A mammal of the quebrada is the tamandua anteater (below). A fully grown adult is about 4 feet (1.2 m) long, including its elongated head and snout, which it uses to

probe ant nests. Tamanduas are adept climbers and use their prehensile tails for grasping branches.

Turtles can be found along Uruguay's coast. The largest is the leatherback.

Turtles

Four species of marine turtles visit the Uruguayan coast. The leatherback, the largest of all turtles, can reach 7 feet (2.1 m) long. The olive ridley is smaller, growing only up to 30 inches (76 cm) long. The Atlantic loggerhead and the green turtle, the largest of the hard-shelled turtles, can reach 39 inches (1 m) long. Green turtles found foraging for marine plants along this coast probably nest on the beaches of Ascension Island, 3,105 miles (4,997 km) away in the Atlantic.

Isla de Lobos

The small Atlantic island of Lobos is about 7.5 miles (12 km) from Punta del Este. *Lobos* is the abbreviated form of *lobos marinos*, which is Spanish for "sea wolves," meaning seals. For several centuries the island was visited only by explorers and pirates. Numerous ships have been wrecked around the island's dangerous shore, and in the mid-nineteenth century a lighthouse was built to guide sailors. The island is named after the masses of seals and sea lions that cover all the space close to the sea. The colony is one of the largest in the Americas. Two species exist side by side: the southern sea lion, with large males reaching about 662 pounds (300 kg), and the smaller South American fur seal, with males growing to about 375 pounds (170 kg). Small numbers of southern elephant seals, which reach about 4,851 pounds (2,200 kg) and are more commonly found in the sub-Antarctic, have been recorded there as well. But like much of the world's wildlife, the seals of Lobos are threatened. At one time it was by hunters looking for skins and oil. Now it is tourism and plans for eco-hotel development on the island that cast a cloud over the future of the colony.

Franciscana River Dolphin

The Franciscana is a unique river dolphin known only in the Río de la Plata region. River dolphins are classified in a different animal family than are sea dolphins. They are often called long-beaked dolphins because of their narrow beaks. The Franciscana's beak, the longest of all river dolphins' beaks, has between fifty and sixty teeth on each side of the upper and lower jaw. Franciscanas feed on small shrimp and other aquatic animals. The origin of the name probably lies in the similarity between the color of the animal and the brown clothes worn by Franciscan friars. The Franciscana is small, only reaching 4.3 to 5.6 feet (1.3–1.7 m) in length, and unfortunately it is easily trapped accidentally in fishing nets. Often the meat is discarded or fed to other animals.

Although the Franciscana is protected in Uruguay, Argentina, and Brazil, the local fishing industry cannot avoid depleting the natural stocks, and very little is known about the size of the population or the habits of the animals. This makes managing the survival of the species difficult, and the only hope is that increasing public and government awareness of conservation will help not only the dolphin but all Uruguayan wildlife.

Conservation Strategy

The Uruguayan Ramsar site that has been given legal protection includes the Parque Nacional Santa Teresa (Saint Teresa National Park) near Laguna Negra. In the park is a preserved eighteenth-century fort. Another part of the protected area is

Saint Teresa National Park is home to a preserved eighteenth-century fort, as well as protected lands.

the fauna refuge of Laguna Castillos, along with the dunes at Cabo Polonia and part of the unusual ombú forest. The ombú tree is a legendary tree of Argentina and Uruguay. Although it is not common and usually grows singly or in small groups, the tree features in paintings, literature, and poetry. It is a relative of the Virginian pokeweed or pigeon-berry found in the

United States and has a large trunk of soft wood that stores water in times of drought. The immense forest close to the Laguna Castillos is the largest group of the trees in the region. Only part of the forest is in the protected zone, though. The majority of the trees are on private land.

The Uruguayan authorities responsible for the Ramsar site also plan to protect a much larger area of adjoining land, which they call Reserva de Biosfera Bañados del Este (Biosphere Reserve of the Eastern Wetlands). A major problem is that much of the land is privately owned. The average size of the landholdings is 988.4 acres (400 ha), and there is extensive cultivation of rice on them. Other areas of the proposed reserve have been planted with introduced pine and eucalyptus trees. The result is that habitats have been fragmented and lost. The authorities would like to encourage measures to slow the process.

Although the natural vegetation has been severely modified by agriculture, one palm native to the area, the butiá (*Butia capitata*), has survived. Also, two smaller plants are on the International Union for the Conservation of Nature Red List of endangered species. One is the dwarf sundew (*Drosera brevifolia*), which has a sticky secretion at the end of hairs on its leaves that snares small insects. When the insects die, they decay, providing the plant with nutrients. The species also grows in parts of the United States, where it is protected by federal and state laws. The other endangered plant is *Cypella herbertii*, a type of iris. The name *Cypella* comes from the form of the flowers, which resemble a cup or a goblet, which is *kypellon* in Greek.

The Banda Oriental

WHEN EUROPEANS FIRST ARRIVED in what is now Uruguay, most of the land was occupied by the Charrúas. This tribe lived by hunting, fishing, and gathering wild fruits and roots. They used bows and arrows, slings, spears, and bolas, which are fiber cords with stones attached to the ends. Thrown from a distance, bolas will wrap around the legs of a bird or another animal, bringing it to the ground.

A typical Charrúa home was made of four poles covered with straw matting. The Charrúas used clay pots for cooking meat and animal hides and furs for clothing. They tattooed their faces with blue vegetable dye, the designs varying by tribe. Tall and big, the Charrúas were aggressive toward other tribes and made surprise attacks on their enemies. It is said they spared the women and children but celebrated their victories by turning the skulls of their male victims into ceremonial drinking cups. They were just as hostile to the first Europeans who arrived in the area.

Native Societies

Andean cultures

Atlantic cultures

Southern cultures

Tropical forest cultures

Charrúa **Native groups**

Present-day boundary

Opposite: **This statue, *The Last of the Charrúas*, by Prati, honors the Charrúa tribe.**

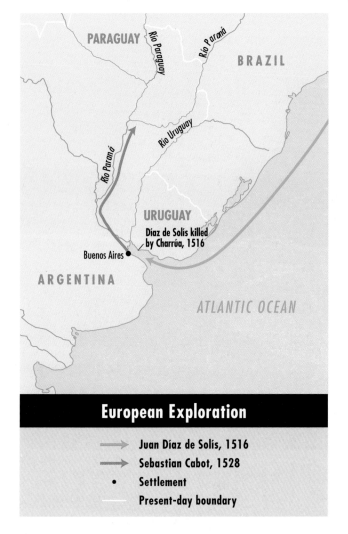

European Exploration

→ Juan Díaz de Solís, 1516
→ Sebastian Cabot, 1528
• Settlement
— Present-day boundary

On the map:
PARAGUAY
Río Paraguay
Río Paraná
BRAZIL
Río Uruguay
Río Paraná
URUGUAY
Díaz de Solís killed by Charrúa, 1516
Buenos Aires
ARGENTINA
ATLANTIC OCEAN

Early in the sixteenth century European explorers were searching for a sea route that connected the Atlantic Ocean with the Pacific Ocean. In 1516, the Spanish explorer Juan Díaz de Solís must have thought he had found it when he sailed into the huge estuary of the Río de la Plata. He and most of his small team were almost immediately ambushed and killed by the Charrúas, but not before they had picked up rumors of silver and gold somewhere upriver. The rumors spread to Europe, but it was ten years before the next expedition set out, led by the English navigator Sebastian Cabot. He established a small settlement called San Salvador in the present-day department of Soriano and spent three years exploring the Río Paraná and the Río Paraguay. But his expedition was not successful. The settlement was destroyed by the Charrúas, and Cabot returned to Europe without a fortune.

Without silver, gold, or other precious minerals, the land to the east of the Río Uruguay, then known as the Banda Oriental, was of no interest to the Europeans. Cabot ignored it, as did the next large expedition, that of the Spaniard Pedro de Mendoza in 1535. In 1536, Mendoza founded Buenos Aires, now the capital of Argentina, and in 1537, he built a fort where Asunción, the capital of Paraguay, now stands. He also was the first person to bring cattle, horses, and pigs to the southern side of the Río de la Plata, where they thrived on the pampas. It was not until more than seventy years later, in 1611, that cattle and horses were introduced into the Banda Oriental. The man behind that visionary act was Hernando Arias, also known as Hernandarias, a locally born governor based in Asunción.

A European explorer, the English navigator Sebastian Cabot, set sail for the South American coast in 1526.

Río de la Plata

The Río de la Plata was named the Río Santa Maria by Juan Díaz de Solís, probably the first European to sail into the estuary, in 1516. After he was killed by the Charrúas, the river was called the Río Solís in his honor. Later it became known as the Río de la Plata, which means "River of Silver" or "River Plate," when explorers, hearing tales of silver and gold upriver, believed the river would lead them to great wealth.

The one hundred cattle and horses that Hernandarias brought to the Banda Oriental proved to be the foundation of Uruguay's agricultural economy. They grew quickly into herds large enough for a leather and hide industry to develop. Cowboys, or gauchos, arrived from Argentina to trade. The Banda Oriental also developed its own gaucho culture, based largely on that of the Charrúas. They proved to be excellent horsemen, and they were used to a nomadic way of life on the plains. They were also hardy, tough, and versatile.

The new industry attracted settlers from Europe who could see the potential of raising cattle in the Banda Oriental. This marked the beginning of real Spanish interest in the colony. Jesuit and Franciscan missionaries also arrived. The purpose behind European exploration of the New World had always been twofold: to acquire wealth and to convert the local people to Catholicism. The missionaries had some success converting the Charrúas, but it was difficult and dangerous work. Spanish control of the colony was challenged by the Portuguese, who already governed the vast

In colonial Uruguay ranches emerged in rural areas, where gauchos raised cattle, and animal skins were made into leather products.

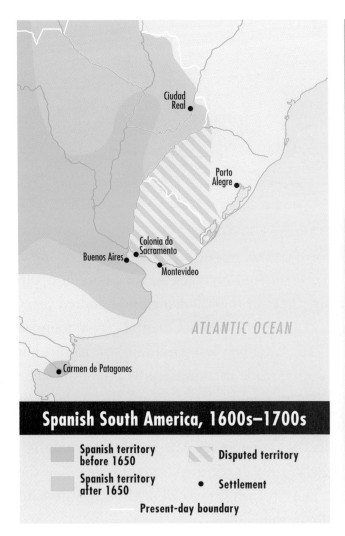

Spanish South America, 1600s–1700s

- Ciudad Real
- Porto Alegre
- Colonia do Sacramento
- Buenos Aires
- Montevideo
- Carmen de Patagones

ATLANTIC OCEAN

- Spanish territory before 1650
- Spanish territory after 1650
- Disputed territory
- ● Settlement
- — Present-day boundary

Colonia del Sacramento was founded in 1680 by the Portuguese to resist the Spanish strategically.

colony of Brazil to the north. The Portuguese wanted to extend Brazil's southern border to the Río de la Plata, and in 1680, they built a settlement at Colonia del Sacramento, on the northern shore of the river, to compete with Buenos Aires on the opposite shore. From this base the Portuguese could disrupt trade between Spain and its colonies in the Río de la

In response to the growing influence of the Portuguese, the Spanish established Montevideo in a sheltered harbor in 1726.

Plata region. This, of course, was unacceptable to the Spanish, and Colonia del Sacramento changed hands between Spain and Portugal many times in the following one hundred years. To strengthen its claim to the Banda Oriental, Spain founded Montevideo in 1726. Initially it was a military stronghold, but its natural harbor soon made it commercially important. The Portuguese and Spanish authorities eventually made their peace in 1776, after the Spanish governor of Buenos Aires destroyed Colonia del Sacramento. The Banda Oriental then became part of the Viceroyalty of the United Provinces of the Río de la Plata. The Spanish crown created viceroyalties to govern its colonies in the New World.

Independence

Early in the nineteenth century Spain faced calls for independence from many of its American colonies. People resented the high taxes imposed by the Spanish government and restrictions that, until 1778, meant the colonies could not trade freely with the rest of the world. Events in Europe helped their cause when the French emperor Napoléon deposed the Spanish king in 1808. In 1810, the Spanish viceroy in Buenos Aires was also removed, and Argentina became independent from Spain in 1816. The situation in the Banda Oriental was more confusing, as there was fighting among the military junta that replaced the Spanish viceroy in Buenos Aires, the Spanish representative in charge of Montevideo, the Portuguese from Brazil, and neighboring

A British Interlude

Great Britain, often a rival of Spain's in Europe, was well aware that by the beginning of the nineteenth century, Spanish control was weakening in the American colonies. In 1806, British military and naval contingents invaded the Río de la Plata estuary, and in 1807, they captured Montevideo (right) to avenge Spain's recapture of Buenos Aires from them. They held the town for only a few months, but knowing that the colonies wanted independence from Spain, they made every effort to encourage the spread of liberal and democratic ideas. They even started a newspaper in Spanish and English called *The Southern Star* in which the issues were openly discussed. British merchants also made the most of their short stay, delighting the local people with fine goods from Europe that the Spaniards previously had banned.

states in Argentina that wanted to annex the territory. Then there were the Orientales themselves, the people of the Banda Oriental, organized under their leader, José Gervasio Artigas.

The fighting lasted many years, and in 1821, Portuguese Brazil annexed the Banda Oriental. Some Orientales who were in exile in Argentina plotted their revenge, and in April 1825, thirty-three of them made a heroic return journey, crossing the Río Uruguay in rowboats. Led by Juan Antonio Lavalleja, and known as the Immortal Thirty-Three, they had the support of the local people in Uruguay and the Argentinian government. Together they forced the Portuguese to withdraw, and in 1828, the Banda Oriental became the República Oriental del Uruguay.

José Gervasio Artigas

The national hero José Gervasio Artigas was born in Montevideo in 1764. His Spanish grandfather had helped to found the city. Artigas was an expert horseman who commanded great loyalty from the men who fought under him in the battle for independence from Spain. He won an early victory in 1811 against the Spanish at Las Piedras. But when events turned against him later in the year, he went into voluntary exile in Argentina. To his surprise, in one of the most extraordinary events of the war, thousands of men, women, children, gauchos, cattle, and oxcarts followed him in what became known as the Exodus. For the first time the Orientales had a real sense of identity as they continued the fight in exile. Artigas continued to lead the struggle until 1820, when he again went into exile in Paraguay, where he stayed until his death in 1850. Today a life-size statue of General Artigas stands above the black marble mausoleum in which he is buried in Plaza Independencia in Montevideo.

Once Uruguay gained independence, two main political parties emerged, the Colorados (Reds) and Blancos (Whites). They were identified by the flags they carried into battle.

Reds and Whites

After independence two opposing sides, the Colorados (Reds) and the Blancos (Whites), dominated the political scene. Initially these were the followers of two generals who carried red and white pennants into battle, but in time Colorados and Blancos represented Uruguay's two main political parties. The leader of the Colorados, General Fructuoso Rivera, became Uruguay's first president (1830–1834). The leader of the Blancos, General Manuel Oribe, succeeded him but was deposed by Rivera, who reinstalled himself as president. Civil war broke out. Generally Montevideo and other towns supported the Colorados, while the Blancos had the backing of the Catholic Church and the wealthy owners of cattle and estates. Each side also got help from other countries: Rivera

South America, 1830

1828 **Date of independence**

from France, Italy, and Great Britain, and Oribe from Argentina. The leader of Argentina was the monstrous dictator General Juan Manuel de Rosas, and it was only after he was deposed in 1852 that fighting stopped in Uruguay.

But not for long. Another Colorado president, General Venancio Flores, came to power in 1865, and because of his close association with Brazil, Uruguay got involved in the devastating War of the Triple Alliance, in which the two countries and Argentina opposed Paraguay. The Colorados held power until the end of the nineteenth century, when rising tensions, revolts, and assassinations led to another civil war.

Developing the Land

At the time Uruguay became an independent republic, it had scarcely 74,000 inhabitants. A few cattle ranchers with large estates controlled most of the country's wealth. Because of the fighting, Uruguay's social and economic development was slow until the last quarter of the nineteenth century, when thousands of immigrants from

Europe arrived. They brought agriculture to the coastal area, and they imported pedigree sheep and cattle, greatly improving the quality of wool and beef. They developed retail trades such as textiles and leather goods. The first textile mill was established in the 1880s.

Gradually foreign companies began to invest in shipping, other commercial activities, and public works. The port of Montevideo was enlarged so that oceangoing vessels could dock for loading and unloading. In 1886, South America's first electric plant was opened in Montevideo. The British built a gasworks there, and the city introduced electric trams. Montevideo's first telephone came into operation in 1878, and by the 1890s the city had more telephones per person than any other South American city. A new railway system meant goods could be transported between Montevideo and other parts of the country quickly.

By the turn of the nineteenth century, Uruguay's economy experienced growth. This photo is of the port in Montevideo c. 1901.

Fray Bentos

Fray Bentos is a small port on the Río Uruguay. Late in the nineteenth century it was the center of a multimillion-dollar trade. The product was Liebig's Extract of Meat. A German named Justus von Liebig (below) conceived of making a meat extract, but the idea was too expensive to carry out in Europe. He needed a place where cattle were cheap and plentiful, and Uruguay was ideal. The business was very successful, and the meat extract sold worldwide. By 1890, however, Liebig's company had expanded into an even more profitable business. Due to the development of canning techniques, the factories at Fray Bentos were able to produce canned corned beef. Millions of cans were sold, especially during the two world wars. At its peak Liebig's Extract of Meat Company employed four thousand people and slaughtered two thousand animals a day. But Liebig's success story did not last, and the machines ground to a halt in 1979.

JUSTUS v. LIEBIG. né en 1803. mort en 1873.

Scènes de la vie de Liebig. 6. Usines de la Comp.ie Liebig à Fray - Bentos.

VÉRITABLE EXTRAIT DE VIANDE LIEBIG.

Voir au verso.

A Welfare State

José Batlle y Ordóñez came to power in 1903 in the midst of a civil war. Since independence, the Colorados or the military had been almost continuously in power. Except for the brief regime of General Oribe, the Blancos had never held office, and they were frustrated. In 1897, Juan Idiarte Borda, the Colorado president, was assassinated. The ensuing war between the Colorados and the Blancos reached its peak in 1904 and resulted in defeat for the Blancos. But President Batlle y Ordóñez ensured a treaty between the two parties that resulted in a long period of peace and orderly government in Uruguay.

The frustrations of the Blancos reflected the state of the country. Most people were poor, uneducated, and living in basic housing. President Batlle y Ordóñez was aware of the conditions, and the years of peace enabled him to introduce reforms. These included labor legislation allowing for an eight-hour working day, one day off for every five worked, the right to strike, accident insurance, and old-age pensions. In the area of economics, he believed that the state should own the country's major industries, including power, communication, insurance, alcohol, and tobacco, and he advised the building of more railways. He also accepted that everyone had a right to be educated and angered the Catholic Church by removing education from its control. Free education was extended to secondary schools and universities, and religious teaching was no longer compulsory. Women were also given the right to file for divorce. These were very radical reforms, and at the time Uruguay had the most advanced social legislation of any Latin American country. Batlle y Ordóñez also tried to introduce some constitutional reform, proposing that the office of president be replaced by a council of nine elected members. But in this he was less successful.

The two world wars (1914–1918 and 1939–1945) benefited Uruguay's economy, as meat and wool were in great demand. They also forced Uruguay to create its own manufacturing industries, as goods often could not be imported from Europe. Good trading conditions brought increased prosperity and helped improve the standard of living for some workers.

The Colorados were still in office after World War II, and they faced many problems. Prices for meat and wool, Uruguay's main exports, dropped on the world market, which led to unemployment and inflation. Uruguay's relations with Argentina, not good during the war, deteriorated further when General Juan Perón was president of Argentina, from 1946 to 1955. Uruguay offered asylum to Argentinian political refugees, while newspapers published and the radio broadcast anti-Perón propaganda. In retaliation President Perón imposed trade restrictions on Uruguay and forbade Argentinians to vacation there. This had a devastating effect on Uruguay's tourism industry.

The *Graf Spee*

A crucial incident in World War II was the sinking of the German battleship *Graf Spee* in Montevideo's harbor. In 1939, the heavily armed ship was attacked by British cruisers and forced into port in Montevideo for repairs. According to war rules, ships were allowed to be in a neutral port for only seventy-two hours. Uruguay at this time had not declared its support for either side and could have helped Germany and its Axis allies by allowing the ship to stay longer. The Uruguayans insisted that the ship leave on time, knowing that British cruisers were waiting for it outside the harbor. Not wishing to face the British ships, the German captain ordered his crew to abandon ship, and it sank into the Río de la Plata. For many years the control tower of the *Graf Spee* could be seen above the water.

The Tupamaros

The guerrilla group the Movimiento de Liberación Nacional, or the Tupamaros, took its name from the last Inca king, Tupac-Amaru. Its aim was to break the power of the ruling classes by armed struggle. Its leader, Raúl Sendic, was a sugar worker from the north who became a law student in Montevideo. He, like many students who joined the struggle, was influenced by the Cuban revolution led by Fidel Castro and Ché Guevara in 1959. For several years the Tupamaros terrorized Uruguay with bombs and shootings. They kidnapped politicians, businessmen, and diplomats. Sometimes the revolutionaries robbed banks and supermarkets and, like modern-day Robin Hoods, distributed their booty to the poor. The Tupamaros kept the country in a state of war until the military crushed the movement in 1972.

Between 1951 and 1966, Uruguay's office of president was abolished and replaced by a nine-member national council with a chairperson chosen from the majority party. In 1958, the Blancos had the most votes for the first time in ninety-three years, but they were unable to stop the decline in the country's fortunes. In 1967, when it was agreed to reinstate the president's office, the Colorados once again won the elections. The situation went from bad to worse. The government tried to impose wage and price controls to halt inflation, but this led to demonstrations, riots, and terrorism. An urban guerrilla group, the Tupamaros, emerged to dominate events in Uruguay for the next few years.

Military Rule

The military defeated the revolutionaries and in 1973 took control of the country's political affairs. The Colorado Juan María Bordaberry had been elected president in 1972. Under pressure from the military, he dissolved Congress and appointed a Council of State with military and civilian

During Juan María Bordaberry's presidency the military overthrew the government to broaden its power.

Government under President Julio María Sanguinetti was known for human rights, democratic, and economic reform.

members. Trade unions were not allowed to demonstrate, and communists and other left-wing groups were banned. The press was heavily censored. Raúl Sendic was sentenced to forty-five years in prison, and thousands of people were secretly detained. In protest at the lack of democratic freedoms, President Bordaberry refused to hold elections in 1976, and the military deposed him. A new military Council of State voted in Aparicio Méndez as president.

Military repression continued. Many thousands of Uruguayans were held as political prisoners, and there was widespread torture. As the number of prisoners grew, the regime was internationally criticized as one of the most repressive in Latin America. Another president, General Gregorio Alvarez, was installed in 1981, but little changed. In desperation the people of Uruguay took to the streets. In 1983, almost 500,000 people took part in a protest in Montevideo. The following year they organized a general strike. The military gave in and agreed to hold elections, with certain conditions, and to restore a civilian government.

Return to Democracy

The successful candidate in the 1984 election was a Colorado moderate, Julio María Sanguinetti. Having won by only a small majority, he formed a government that included members of other parties. Various outlawed organizations, including the Communist party, were made legal, and new laws allowed for all of Uruguay's political prisoners and thousands of common criminals to be released. Sanguinetti's government also proposed amnesty for all military and police personnel involved in crimes against humanity during the military dictatorship. Left-wing groups, trade unions, and student groups were opposed to the amnesty and forced a referendum on the issue. The majority of the people, anxious for peace, law, and order and eager to get the country back on its feet, backed the president.

Economic conditions in Uruguay continued to be very bad, and workers called frequent strikes. There were two twenty-four-hour-long general strikes in 1989, the year Luis Alberto Lacalle Herrera was elected president. Herrera was a member of the Blancos, now known as the National Party, and this was their first victory since 1958.

Luis Alberto Lacalle Herrera did not have a working majority in the Congress and he had to form a coalition with the Colorado party. The Colorados agreed that in return for four of their members being appointed to the Council of State, they would support the Blancos' legislation for economic reform. This included transferring state-owned companies to the private sector, reducing government spending, encouraging foreign investment, and renegotiating debts owed by Uruguay to foreign governments and banks. Uruguayan workers, fearful of increased unemployment, higher taxes, and cuts in government spending of social and medical benefits, responded to this program with general strikes and protests.

Governing the Country

THE BROAD FRONT IS A COALITION OF LEFT-WING PARTIES that was formed in 1971. It includes communists, socialists, and former Tupamaro guerrillas. With Uruguay under military rule between 1973 and 1985, it was difficult for the Broad Front to operate, as various parties were banned, and some members were not allowed to stand for election. However, the Broad Front did well in the 1984 elections, winning 21 percent of the vote, even though its first-choice candidate had been barred from taking part.

A significant factor in its success was the support it received from the people of Montevideo. Five years later the Montevideans elected the Broad Front candidate Tabaré Vásquez to be the city's mayor. In 1994, Vásquez was the Broad Front's candidate in the national elections. Although the elections were won by Julio María Sanguinetti, who took

Opposite: **Uruguay's flag flies before the Palacio Legislativo (Legislative Palace).**

The National Flag

The national flag originated in 1830. It has nine alternating blue and white stripes that represent the provinces into which the country was divided after gaining independence. In the top left corner is a golden sun with sixteen rays that are alternately triangular and wavy. This Sun of May symbolizes Uruguay's independence.

up his second term in office, the results were very close. The Colorados gained 31.4 percent of the vote, the National Party (Blancos) 30.2 percent, and the Broad Front 30 percent. In recent years there has been much infighting between the parties of the Broad Front, which has threatened to undermine its position as a viable third political party.

In the 1999 presidential election Tabaré Vásquez actually won the first round, defeating the Colorado and National Party candidates. The Colorado candidate Jorge Batlle Ibáñez emerged the winner, but only after gaining the support of the Blancos. The Broad Front, which changed its name to the Progressive Encounter coalition, had the majority of seats in both houses of Congress. It was the main opposition party and campaigned for economic, social, and educational improvements and a fairer distribution of wealth among the people.

Presidential candidate Tabaré Vásquez casts his vote in the 1999 presidential election.

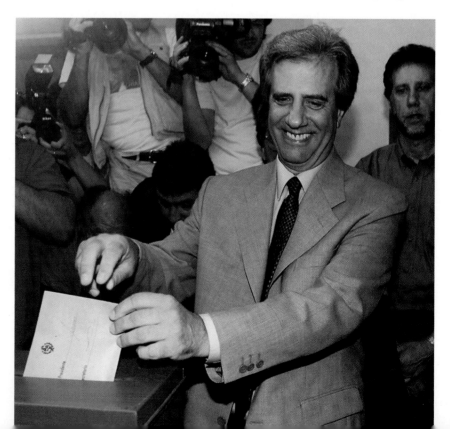

President Jorge Batlle Ibáñez waves to supporters after winning the 2000 presidential election.

Uruguay Today

The first years of the new millennium were tough for the economies of the Plate region, especially for Argentina, and President Jorge Batlle Ibáñez did not come up to voters' expectations. The recession left one-third of Uruguayans below the poverty line and forced 100,000 mostly young people to emigrate. The Progressive Encounter candidate Tabaré Vásquez won the 2004 election, though with a lower margin than expected in view of the poor standing of the outgoing president.

José Batlle y Ordóñez

José Batlle y Ordóñez (1856–1929) was twice president of Uruguay (1903–1907 and 1911–1915). He was a great statesman and one of Latin America's most forward-thinking social reformers. The son of a previous president, Lorenzo Batlle y Grau, he was born in Montevideo and became a successful journalist. At age thirty he founded the daily newspaper *El día* and used it as a forum for discussing the nation's problems. He was a senator from 1896 to 1903 and leader of the Colorados. He was a man acutely aware of the great gap between the rich and the poor in his country. Between his presidencies he studied social and political ideas in Europe, which he brought back to Uruguay. His social reforms were outstanding, and he will be remembered as the man who introduced a welfare state, the first in Latin America, to Uruguay.

The challenge for the new president is clear. Jobs are needed and his coalition with its leftist mix of radicals, reformers, and ex-guerrillas has to gain the confidence of international investors. When accepting the presidency Tabaré Vásquez said he would not allow Uruguay to default on its international debt and instead he would promote growth in the economy by attracting investment. He will have to balance the economic policies required by investors and the ideals of the coalition. But in modern Latin America, Tabaré Vásquez is in good company with the left-leaning administrations of his neighbors.

Inside the Legislative Palace, the two chambers of Congress meet.

The Constitution

Uruguay's present constitution dates from 1966, though reforms have been made to it since. According to the constitution the president and the vice president are elected on the same ticket by popular vote for a five-year term. Neither can be reelected until five years after completion of their first terms in office. Every citizen over the age of eighteen must vote. The president is the head of government and the commander of the armed forces. The president and the vice president must be over thirty-five years old and citizens of Uruguay. They exercise executive power with a Council of Ministers, appointed by the president with approval of Congress. Responsibilities of the Council of Ministers include foreign

National Anthem

Uruguay's national anthem, "Orientales, la patria o la tumba" ("Orientales, the Fatherland or Death") was adopted in 1845. It has eleven verses. The words are by Francisco Esteban Acuña de Figueroa (1791–1862), and the music is by Francisco José Debali (1791–1859).

Orientales, our nation or the grave,
Liberty or with glory we die.
It's the vows that our souls pronounce
And which heroically we will fulfill.

Liberty, liberty, Orientales.
This is the outcry which our nation saved
And its braves in fierce battles
Of sublime enthusiasm enflamed.

This holy gift of glory we deserved
Tyrants: Tremble!
Liberty in combat we will cry out!
And even dying, freedom we shall also shout!

affairs, national defense, economy and finance, education, and tourism.

Legislative power lies with Congress, which consists of a Chamber of Senators and a Chamber of Representatives. There are thirty senators and ninety-nine representatives, each elected by popular vote for five years. The representatives are elected by the nineteen departments of Uruguay, with each department having at least two representatives.

Judicial power is vested in the Supreme Court. Members of the Supreme Court, who must be between forty and seventy years of age, are nominated by the president and elected by Congress for ten-year terms. The Supreme Court members appoint all other judges and law officials. Lower courts include appellate courts, or courts of appeal; courts of first instance, which deal with criminal, civil, and labor matters; and justice of the peace courts, where judgments are made on small-claims cases and local issues.

The constitution also states that 25 percent of the electorate can force a referendum to reconsider a law passed by Congress. There have been thirteen referendums since 1917. The most recent, in 1989, supported

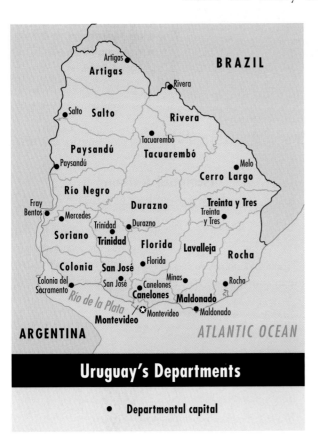

Uruguay's Departments

• **Departmental capital**

President Sanguinetti's granting amnesty to military officers accused of human-rights abuses.

Uruguay has nineteen departments. Each has a governor and, with the exception of Montevideo, a departmental board with thirty-one members. Montevideo has more than sixty departmental board members. The governors and the members of the board are elected for five years. The boards are responsible for public services, public health, and education within their regions.

NATIONAL GOVERNMENT OF URUGUAY

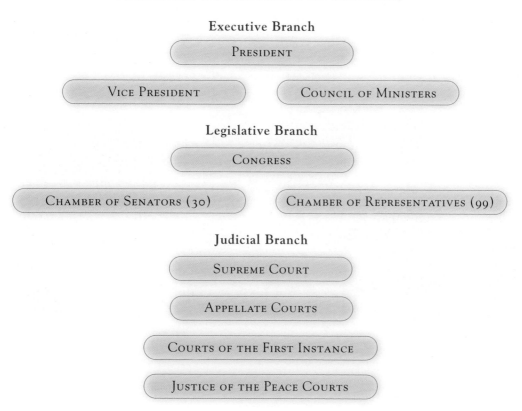

Executive Branch

PRESIDENT

VICE PRESIDENT   COUNCIL OF MINISTERS

Legislative Branch

CONGRESS

CHAMBER OF SENATORS (30)   CHAMBER OF REPRESENTATIVES (99)

Judicial Branch

SUPREME COURT

APPELLATE COURTS

COURTS OF THE FIRST INSTANCE

JUSTICE OF THE PEACE COURTS

Montevideo: Did You Know This?

The historic section of Montevideo lies within just a few blocks of the port. The oldest square is Plaza de la Constitución, also known as Plaza Matriz. On one side of the square stands the Metropolitan Cathedral, built between 1790 and 1804, and on the other is the old town hall, or *el Cabildo*, also built in 1804, where the independence of Uruguay was plotted. In a small square nearby is a statue of the founder of the city, Bruno Mauricio de Zabala. Montevideo has expanded many miles beyond the old city and now includes residential and industrial suburbs, shopping streets, a financial center, many parks full of trees, and miles of beautiful beaches.

Population (2004 est.): 1,346,900
Year Founded: 1726, by Bruno Mauricio de Zabala
Altitude: sea level
Average Daily Temperature: January 72°F (22°C), July 50°F (10°C)
Average Annual Rainfall: 37.4 inches (95 cm)

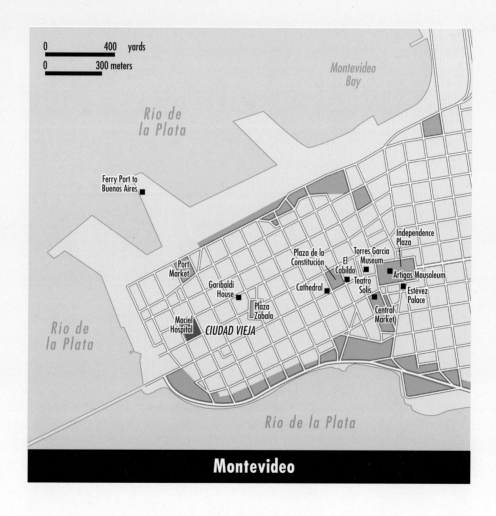

Montevideo

An
Agricultural
Economy

I

N 1991, URUGUAY WAS A FOUNDING MEMBER OF MERCOSUR, the Southern Cone Common Market, with Argentina, Brazil, and Paraguay. A common market allows each member unrestricted trade with the other members. This adds up to a potential market of more than 200 million people. Uruguay's main exports are meat, wool, and hides, more than half of which go to Argentina and Brazil. Other trading partners include the United States, the European Union, China, and other countries in South America. From 1996 to 1998, Uruguay's economy had an average annual growth of about 5 percent, which was good, but by the beginning of the twenty-first century, its economy was in deep trouble.

Opposite: **Though most of Uruguay's land is used for the raising of cattle and sheep, a small percentage is used for growing crops.**

People at Work

Sixty-six percent of Uruguayans work in service industries. These include government agencies, financial institutions, education and health care, transportation, and communication. Also, many people work for the tourism industry, in hotels and restaurants. Twenty-six percent of workers are employed in industry, the majority in the manufacturing sector, and 7.4 percent in agriculture, fishing, and forestry.

Uruguay's economic problems are closely related to those in neighboring Argentina and Brazil. In 1999 Brazil had to devalue its currency, which meant that imports from Uruguay became more expensive, so Brazil bought less. Two years later Argentina's problems were bordering on disaster, as the country was running out of money. For many days its banks were closed, and people demonstrated in the streets, demanding their wages and access to their bank accounts. Argentinians began to withdraw huge amounts of cash from bank accounts they held in Uruguay. Sensing a panic, Uruguayans did the same, leaving the Uruguayan banks almost without money. The government remedied the situation by borrowing from international financial institutions. Meanwhile, the tourism industry was badly hit. Most visitors to Uruguay are Argentinians and Brazilians, but many could no longer afford vacations. Other reasons for the decline in Uruguay's economy included an outbreak of foot-and-mouth disease among cattle in 2001, which reduced beef exports to North America, and a drop in world prices for meat and wool.

Between 1999 and 2002, the total gross domestic

People wait in line at a bank entrance in Montevideo to withdraw their money.

Currency

On March 1, 1993, the Uruguayan government introduced a new currency: the new peso, the equivalent of 1,000 old pesos. In 1998, 10.47 new pesos equalled US$1. But by December 2004, it took 26.30 new pesos to equal US$1.

The 5-peso note carries an image of Joaquín Torres-García, one of Uruguay's greatest artists, who died in 1949. He created a form of abstract art called constructivism, which uses many signs and symbols. An

example of his work, *Pintura Constructiva*, painted in 1943, is on the reverse side of the note.

product (GDP)—that is, the total value of all goods and services produced in the country each year—dropped by nearly 20 percent. Unemployment rose to 16.1 percent in 2003, and inflation increased from about 4 percent in 2001 to 26 percent in 2002. Inflation makes goods more expensive, so people buy less, and that hurts the economy. Uruguay also has the problem, shared by many developing countries, of owing billions of dollars to international banks, governments, and institutions. To continue to receive more loans, which it needs to keep the country going, the government has to agree to some strict conditions. These include cuts in government spending and higher taxation, measures that make life even harder for ordinary Uruguayan workers.

Livestock

Uruguay's grass-covered hills and plains are ideal for raising cattle and sheep, and more than three-quarters of the land is given over to pasture. There is also plenty of water and a

More than three-quarters of Uruguay's land is available for its great number of livestock.

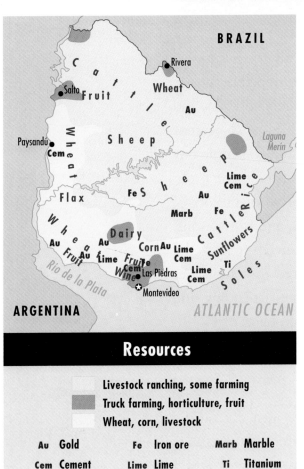

BRAZIL

Rivera

Salto

Fruit

Wheat

Au

Paysandú

Wheat

Sheep

Laguna Merin

Cem

Flax

Fe S

Sheep

Au

Lime Cem

Marb

Fe

Wheat

Dairy

Corn Au

Cattle Rice

Au

Au

Lime

Au

Lime Fruit

Cem

Sunflowers

Río de la Plata

Wine

Cem Las Piedras

Lime Cem

Ti

Soles

Montevideo

ARGENTINA

ATLANTIC OCEAN

Resources

- Livestock ranching, some farming
- Truck farming, horticulture, fruit
- Wheat, corn, livestock

Au Gold	Fe Iron ore	Marb Marble
Cem Cement	Lime Lime	Ti Titanium

mostly mild climate. Parts of the country are occasionally affected by drought, however. In 1988–1989 in the north, for instance, more than 650,000 cattle died or had to be killed because of a drought. In 2002, Uruguay had 13 million sheep, 11.7 million cattle, more than 500,000 horses, and almost 400,000 hogs. Beef cattle are mainly Herefords. Sheep breeds include Corriedale, which is valued for its meat, and crossbreed for their wool. Sheep far outnumber cattle in the northwest, but cattle are of major importance south of the Río Negro.

The agriculture industry employs about 14 percent of the workforce and in 2000 accounted for more than 40 percent of exports in the form of live animals, meat, wool, and hides. Uruguay also has a dairy industry and in 1998 was the world's tenth greatest exporter of milk.

Crops

In Uruguay only about 7 percent of the land is used for growing crops. Rice is the most important crop. It is grown mostly in the departments of Cerro Largo, Treinta y Tres, and Rocha, where its production is closely connected to raising livestock. Ranchers find that they can use land to grow rice for a couple of years, then sow the same land with grass for four or five years to provide pasture for cattle. Most of the rice is grown for export. Other exports include barley, soybeans, and oil crops such as flaxseeds and sunflower seeds. Wheat and sugar are important food crops for the home market, while corn is used mostly as animal feed.

One important crop in Uruguay is sunflowers. Their seeds are exported to other countries.

Grapes await harvesting at this vineyard.

Citrus and produce farms around Montevideo supply the city with fruits and vegetables, and Uruguay exports oranges, lemons, and grapefruits. There are many orchards around Salto, which is another center for growing and processing oranges and other citrus fruits. Uruguay has a young but thriving wine industry based mainly on vineyards in the south, close to Montevideo. The first vines were introduced by European immigrants in the 1870s, but only in the past thirty years has there been a real drive to make good wine and export it.

Forestry and Fishing

Uruguay's forestry and fishing industries are small. Less than 4 percent of the land is covered with native forest. There are plantations that grow mainly eucalyptus and pine, but most of the wood is used for fuel.

The government-supported fishing fleet catches hake, croaker, weakfish, and anchovy off the Atlantic coast. Most is for export, as there is little demand for fish in the local market.

Industry

About a quarter of Uruguayan workers are employed in industry, which includes manufacturing and construction. Most of the country's factories are in industrial suburbs close to Montevideo, where pollution is now becoming a problem. Not surprisingly the nation's manufacturing is based on the livestock and agricultural industries. The main products are processed foods, especially meat, dairy foods, sugar, and wine, along with woolen, cotton, and rayon textiles and leather

What Uruguay Grows and Makes

Crops (2000 est.)

Rice	1,175,000 metric tons
Wheat	310,000 metric tons
Barley	200,000 metric tons

Livestock Products (2000 est.)

Beef and veal	453,000 metric tons
Raw wool	55,000 metric tons
Lamb and mutton	51,000 metric tons

Manufacturing

Cement (1997)	781 metric tons
Sugar (1998)	14 metric tons

Leather goods are a main export product in Uruguay.

goods. Other factories manufacture items such as cement, plywood, vehicle tires, and chemicals. Uruguay also has car and truck assembly plants and an oil refinery. Construction workers have been busy in recent years building hotels and tourist facilities, especially in Punta del Este.

Many Uruguayan industries belong to private companies. But others, such as insurance, electrical power, oil refining, telephone, and the national airline, have traditionally been owned by the government. Now there are plans to privatize several of these industries, although left-wing groups are opposed to the idea.

Mining

Uruguay has few known mineral resources. Construction materials such as sand, clay, limestone, and granite are the main mineral products. Granite is used in the ornamental rock industry, and Uruguay exports it worldwide. Small amounts of gold and silver are mined, and exploration is under way to find diamonds.

Semiprecious stones, such as agates and amethysts, are mined in the north. Uruguayan amethysts, with their distinct deep violet color, are considered to be of high quality and are exported. The semiprecious stones are also fashioned for sale in tourist shops in Montevideo and Punta del Este.

Energy

Uruguay does not have its own supplies of coal, oil, and natural gas, so it imports large quantities of these fuels for industrial and domestic use. The country relies almost entirely on hydroelectric power for its electricity. Power plants on the Río Uruguay and the Río Negro supply electricity to all parts of the country.

The largest power plant is the Salto Grande on the Río Uruguay, built jointly with Argentina and completed in 1982. Hydroelectricity production varies greatly depending on rainfall, however, and during times of drought, Uruguay has had to import power from Argentina and Brazil. At other times power production has exceeded demand, allowing Uruguay to export electricity to its neighbors. There are plans to increase the use of natural gas from Argentina, and the first pipeline began operating between the two countries in 1998.

Roadways in Uruguay are in good condition. This is Route 9, which runs through the Cuchilla Grande.

Transport

Uruguay has a good road network that connects Montevideo to most other parts of the country. Many people own cars but prefer to travel long distances by bus services, which are efficient and comfortable. By contrast the rail services are slow and very limited. In some rural towns goods are still delivered by horse and cart.

Montevideo is the country's major port and handles about 90 percent of the country's imports and exports. Other ports include Punta del Este, and on the Río Uruguay, Colonia del Sacramento, Fray Bentos, Paysandú, and Salto. There are international airports in Montevideo and Punta del Este.

Tourism

About 80 percent of tourists who visit Uruguay come from Argentina, and about 10 percent come from Brazil. Visitors from other parts of the world are few, perhaps because of the many better-known attractions South America has to offer. Even so, tourism is an important part of the Uruguayan economy, and in 2000 more than 2 million people visited the country. The revenue derived from tourism that year was US$652 million.

Tourism plays a large part in Uruguay's economy, generating over $650 million per year.

The main attractions for tourists are the beautiful sandy beaches and woodlands on the coast; the interior grasslands with their variety of animals and plants; the historic town of Colonia del Sacramento, now a World Heritage site, and the Río Uruguay.

Punta del Este

Punta del Este, Uruguay's major resort, is some 86 miles (138 km) east of Montevideo on the south coast. It is built on a narrow peninsula facing the Río de la Plata on one side and the Atlantic Ocean on the other. The peninsula is covered with hotels and apartment blocks, though close to the tip of the promontory, none are allowed to be taller than the historic lighthouse, El Faro. Behind the peninsula the land is covered with eucalyptus and pine trees. The beaches of Punta del Este are of magnificent, white sand with the clear water of the Playa Mansa beach on the Río de la Plata side, and rough, rocky beaches and coves on the Atlantic side. In recent years Punta del Este has become popular with celebrities from the United States and Europe, and there are some grand vacation homes in the area. It also boasts a fine yacht club. The high season is from December to February, when the resort is packed with visitors. But for much of the rest of the year, the eight thousand year-round inhabitants have the place to themselves.

People of Uruguay

ALMOST 3.5 MILLION PEOPLE LIVE IN URUGUAY, AND more than 90 percent of them live in towns. Uruguay is the most urbanized country in South America. Almost half of the population lives in Montevideo, the only really large city, and most of the other half in the twenty or so small towns that are scattered over the country. Except for Salto, none of the other towns have more than 100,000 people. Uruguay is described as one of the least densely populated countries in South America, with an average of just 50 people per square mile (18 people per sq km), but the distribution of the population is clearly very uneven.

Uruguayans are predominantly white, many with blond hair and blue eyes. The whites are largely descended from immigrants and account for about 88 percent of the population. About 8 percent of the people are mestizos, or people of mixed European and Native American parentage, and 4 percent are Afro-Uruguayans, mixed-race descendents of black African slaves and white Europeans.

Opposite: **Uruguayans are a mixed people with ancestors of Native American, black, and European descent.**

Who Lives in Uruguay?

Whites	88%
Mestizos	8%
Blacks	4%

Though not a densely populated country, Uruguay hosts 3.5 million people.

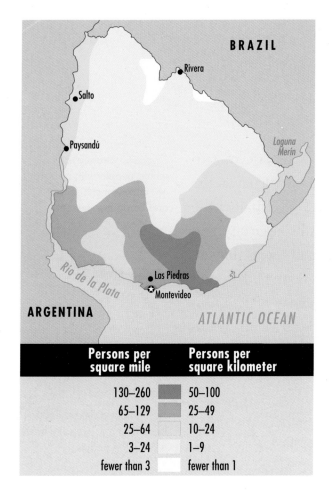

Persons per square mile		Persons per square kilometer
130–260		50–100
65–129		25–49
25–64		10–24
3–24		1–9
fewer than 3		fewer than 1

The Last of the Charrúas

By the end of the eighteenth century, there were almost no Charrúas left. From the time the Spaniards and other explorers arrived, their days were numbered. They took to the gaucho life, but as estancias were created there was tension between the landowners and the native people. The landowners wanted to drive them off the land, and the Charrúas retaliated by raiding the herds and stealing cattle. There were frequent battles. The Charrúas also died from diseases such as smallpox, measles, yellow fever, and malaria, which the Europeans had unwittingly introduced. At the same time, because many Europeans arrived without women, they bred with the Charrúas, giving rise to the mixed-race mestizo population. As the mestizo population grew in size, the Charrúa population declined.

Some more fortunate Charrúas were taken into the Jesuit and Franciscan missions, where they worked the land and were well fed and looked after if they were sick. Some learned to read and write, to paint, and even to play music, and the women were taught to weave. But this protection came to an end when the missionaries were expelled from South America in 1767. Today there is a bronze statue called *The Last of the Charrúas* in a park in Montevideo. Four members of a family, men in typical dress and a woman holding her baby, sit with sad expressions around a hearth.

Immigrants

In the troubled years immediately after Uruguay gained its independence, the population remained at about 74,000 people. But by the end of the century, the number had increased almost to one million. At first there was only a trickle of immigrants, mostly from Europe. But after 1875, when the country was more peaceful, hundreds of thousands arrived—so many, in fact, that the story went that when asked where they "descended from," Uruguayans would answer, "From boats." Most immigrants came from Italy, Spain, and other parts of Europe. Many Italians and Spaniards came from towns and did not take readily to a life of cattle ranching. Instead they set themselves up in small trading concerns, in import and export firms, and in shipping.

Others preferred commercial farming and cultivated small plots, mostly around Montevideo. The population of the department of Montevideo grew from 58,000 in 1860 to 300,000 by 1908. The immigrants also developed small farms along the coast, producing fruits and vegetables that were common in the Mediterranean countries they had left. German families who arrived around 1850 set up estancias in the southern and western regions. They founded small villages such as Nuevo Berlín in Río Negro Province, and in 1857 they built a German Evangelist church with its own school in Montevideo.

Population of Major Cities (2004 est.)

Montevideo	1,346,900
Salto	103,800
Paysandú	78,700
Las Piedras	73,000
Rivera	67,800

British immigrants came mainly from Scotland and England, and they became involved in the cattle industry. They too went to the fertile province of the Río Negro, where they created estancias and imported herds of pedigree cattle and sheep. The town of Young is named after an English cabinetmaker. He was commissioned to carve doors for the new cathedral, and when the job was finished, he and a friend bought land and settled down. Their estancia is still well known for breeding fine cattle and sheep. The British also got involved in constructing railroads and gasworks, and they built a British school and hospital in Montevideo. They even opened a cricket club, and one beach is still known as the *Playa de los Ingleses*, or English Beach.

Immigrants continued to arrive in the early twentieth century. Many were fleeing from troubles in their own countries.

This woman displays handicrafts in San Javier, home to Russian immigrants.

They included Poles, Romanians, Russians, Turks, and Lebanese, as well as Jewish refugees from Germany. A group of Mennonites arrived from Poland at the outbreak of World War II and founded a farming community at Colonia El Ombú, near the town of Young. San Javier, a village on the Río Uruguay south of Paysandú, is home to the descendents of Russian immigrants who still live in some respects like their grandparents did. They use horse-drawn carts to transport people and produce, and fishermen on the river use rowboats similar to those found in the Danube delta. Many of the people retain Russian names, though intermarriage has added some Spanish. In 2003, at least two of the original colonists were still alive, one of them 101 years old and the other 97.

All these nationalities have merged to create a nation of Uruguayans. But the population has grown more slowly than those of most other Latin American countries, and a larger percentage of the population is elderly. The average life expectancy is seventy-five years, compared with seventy-one years in Brazil. It is a matter of some concern, therefore, that during the past twenty years, an estimated 500,000 people, many of them young, have emigrated. They have left mainly for economic and political reasons. Most go to Spain, Argentina, and the United States.

Colonia Suiza

Route 1 is the main road that connects Montevideo and Colonia del Sacramento. Just off the road at kilometer 121 is the town of Colonia Suiza, which is also known as Nueva Helvecia, or "New Switzerland." The name originates from the Swiss immigrants who founded the town in 1862. They were very hardworking and devoted their efforts to creating a leading rural community. They began a dairy industry, cultivated fruit, grew wheat for the mills in Montevideo, and were the first to import a threshing machine. Today Colonia Suiza is at the heart of Uruguay's dairy industry. It is particularly well known for its excellent cheeses. This photo shows a shop owner with fresh cheese for sale. The community does not forget its Swiss origins. The tourist shops sell music boxes and cuckoo clocks, and on August 1 everyone takes the day off to celebrate Swiss National Day.

Some Afro-Uruguayans live in the Barrio Sur suburb of Montevideo.

Afro-Uruguayans

In the late 1700s and through the 1800s, Montevideo was an important port for the African slave trade. Slaves brought mainly from West Africa arrived in Buenos Aires and Montevideo, and most were then transported to other parts of the continent. Today's Afro-Uruguayans are descendents of slaves and European immigrants. Some live in suburbs of Montevideo such as Barrio Sur. Most have moved south from Brazil and live near the border in the north.

Afro-Uruguayans rehearse dances for carnival.

Although only a tiny minority of the population, historically they have had a considerable impact on the literature and music of the country. From 1936 to 1944, they also had their own political party, one of only three black political parties in Latin America. Currently they have one of the leading black civil-rights organizations in Latin America, Mundo Afro (African World), which they founded in 1989.

Common Words and Phrases

adiós (ah-dee-OHS)	good-bye
buenos días (BWAHN-ohs DEE-yahs)	good morning
buenos noches (BWAHN-ohs NOH-ches)	good evening/good night
cuánto? (KWAHN-toh)	how much?
cuantos? (KWAHN-tohs)	how many?
dónde esta? (DOHN-day ess-TAH)	where is?
gracias (GRAH-see-ash)	thank you
no (nah)	no
por favor (pohr fah-VOHR)	please
sí (see)	yes

Language

Spanish is the official language of Uruguay. All native languages have disappeared, but in towns close to the Brazilian border, people speak a mix of Portuguese and Spanish. The slang is known as Portuñol—from "Portuguese" and "español," the Spanish word for "Spanish."

The Spanish alphabet has twenty-eight letters. Consonants are mostly similar to those in English, with some exceptions. Spanish does not pronounce *k* or *w*, but it does include the sounds *ch*, as in "charm"; *ll* like the *y* in "yellow"; *ñ* as in "onion"; and *rr*, well rolled. Other differences in pronunciation include *b*, which sounds like *v*; *c*, which before *e* and *i* is pronounced like *c*; *d*, which within a word is pronounced *th*, except after *l* and *n*, when it is pronounced *d*; *h*, which is not pronounced; *j*, which sounds like *h* in "hello"; and *qu*, which sounds like *k*.

Gauchos

Tourists in Uruguay are encouraged to visit estancias to see the traditional way of life and watch gauchos at work. Gauchos are part of the history and folklore of Uruguay, and they are known for their courage. The Charrúas were the first gauchos. They were joined, and ultimately replaced, by immigrants who for one reason or another did not want to live and work in the coastal areas of the country. Some were criminals; others just preferred a rural lifestyle. Cattle provided gauchos with everything they needed: food, transportation, and leather for saddles, clothing, sacks, and wineskins. The gauchos' independence of spirit, self-sufficiency, and toughness, along with their expert horsemanship, made them invaluable fighters, and many fought hard for General Artigas during the wars of independence.

Gauchos have played a major role in Uruguay's history and culture.

The traditional dress of a gaucho is a broad-brimmed black hat, a long-sleeve cotton shirt, baggy trousers called *bombachas*, black leather boots, and a large poncho for cold weather. A gaucho also has two essential pieces of equipment: his knife, or *facón*, which is tucked inside his leather belt, and a lasso. A gaucho is also never without his cup of *yerba maté*, which is like a green herbal tea.

This gaucho wears many items of traditional gaucho dress.

During the years the gaucho's life has changed, and he no longer roams as freely as he did. Estancias have been fenced off and reduced in size, and the sheep and cattle are kept within the fences. Being a gaucho is still hard work, though. The days are long, as gauchos round up the animals for the slaughterhouse, brand them, mend fences, and break in wild young horses. Today this way of life no longer appeals to many young men, who prefer to look for work in the towns.

A *jineteada* is a traditional gaucho folklore festival. The main attraction is wild-horse riding, rather like bronco riding in the United States. The *jinetes* ride either bareback or with saddles, but on horses three to four years old that have never been ridden before. An equally traditional part of the festival is the *asado* in which whole sides of beef, still with their hides on, are barbecued over hot coals for many, many hours.

Freedom of Faiths

94

In many parts of South America, the rich folklore and oral tradition of the native people has carried some of their early religious beliefs forward to the present day. In Uruguay the Charrúas have been gone for a long time, and little is known about their religious ideas. The Spanish and Portuguese colonists introduced the Catholic religion, which dominated spiritual life until the time of President Batlle y Ordóñez. From 1917 onward Uruguay became secular, with separation of the church and state. Very few visible remains have survived from the times when the church was powerful, and even the mission centers founded in the seventeenth century are no more than glorious ruins. The missions became part of Brazil during the independence wars, and the ruins are now a World Heritage site. Known as the Seven Villages of the Missions of the Oriental, they lie about 186 miles (300 km) north of the border.

Opposite: **Freedom of religion is granted to all Uruguayans. This is the Nuestra Señora del Candelaria church in Punta del Este.**

One Christian denomination in Uruguay is the Mennonite Church.

Freedom of Religion

The Uruguayan constitution allows for total religious freedom, and it is against the law to discriminate against any religion. Religious instruction is not taught in schools, though private schools belonging mainly to the Catholic and Jewish communities cater to their special needs. Many immigrants brought their faiths from their

Catholic	52%
Protestant	16%
No religious preference	16%
Atheist or agnostic	13%
Jewish	2%
Other	1%

homelands, and some are fervent in their beliefs. Others are nominally Catholic but do not practice their religion.

National holidays are seldom religious holidays. Easter Week has become the Semana Criolla, with outdoor barbecues, folk music, and horse breaking. Las Llamadas, or Carnival, the week before Lent, is a fun time with music and dancing. Christmas is celebrated more traditionally, and the nativity scene, or *pesebre*, plays an important part in homes and churches. Families get together for a meal, to open presents, and celebrate, while some attend midnight mass on Christmas Eve.

Catholics and Protestants

The Catholic churches in Uruguay are mostly empty, with declining numbers of people attending Mass. In 1978, the church body known as the Uruguayan Bishops Conference reported that only 105,248 Uruguayans attended Mass regularly. At the time this figure represented just 4 percent of the population. Other surveys showed that more women, mostly from wealthier families, than men attended Mass.

Most Uruguayans do not attend church.

Most of the Protestant minority follow the Anglican, Methodist, Lutheran, and Baptist religions. The Anglican Church in Uruguay began work in 1844 in Montevideo and Salto. At the start it served the English communities but has since developed to embrace other Uruguayans. In 1988, the church became an independent diocese, or region, under the care of its own bishop, and took a lead with numerous social projects. Among the other Christian denominations, or religious bodies with a specific name, there are Evangelicals, Pentecostals, Mennonites, Eastern Orthodox, Jehovah's Witnesses, and Mormons. The Mormons, members of the Church of Jesus Christ of Latter-Day Saints, have a following of around 65,000.

For many years missionaries and radio broadcasts spread religious messages to South America. Now the Internet has entered the picture, and Evangelical churches have well-constructed Web sites. But while the number of Protestants has increased in other South American countries, especially in parts of neighboring Brazil, the Uruguayans have not been quick to follow.

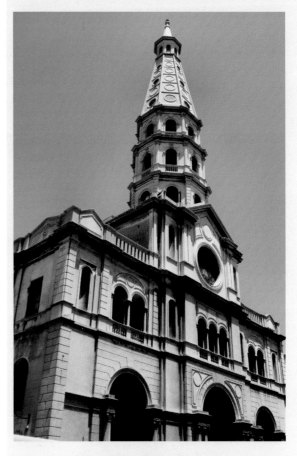

The Catedral Matriz

The Catedral Matriz (Metropolitan Cathedral) in Montevideo is one of the landmarks of the old city. It is also known as the Iglesia Matriz. Construction started in 1790 under the direction of a Portuguese military engineer and was continued by the architect Tomás Toribio in an austere, neoclassic Spanish style. The cathedral took fourteen years to complete, and its facade has been altered twice: once in 1860 and again halfway through the twentieth century.

The Russians of San Javier

July 27, 2003, was the ninetieth anniversary of the founding of the small community of Russians in San Javier alongside the Río Uruguay. Their religious background goes back to troubled times in Russia at the end of the nineteenth century, when many splits occurred in the Russian Orthodox Church, and numerous sects appeared. One of these sects was known as New Israel, a name derived from the idea that its followers were chosen by God.

Russian immigrants in San Javier stand outside a New Israel church.

The leader of the sect was a young man named Vasilli Lubakov, and he took his followers from Russia to Uruguay, where they were welcomed in the reformed secular state. The people of San Javier maintain many Russian traditions, including marriage feasts with music and dancing.

The Jewish Community

Approximately ten thousand families in Uruguay are Jewish, and most of them live in Montevideo. Several hundred live in Paysandú, while others are scattered in the smaller towns. Their history in Uruguay dates back to 1880.

German president Johannes Rau (left) and former Uruguayan president Jorge Batlle Ibáñez light a candle at a B'nai B'rith Jewish organization in Monevideo.

Many families arrived because Uruguay was a stopping place on the route from their homelands to Argentina or Brazil. By 1918, there were 1,700 Jews in the country, mostly Sephardim from countries around the Mediterranean. Later immigrants arrived from Germany, Poland, Hungary, and Russia. By the 1950s, the Jewish community numbered about fifty thousand.

Today the Jewish community is made of up four religious communities: Polish-Russian, Sephardim, German, and Hungarian. Four Jewish schools offer curricula in both Hebrew and Spanish, and several vocational schools provide special training. There are fourteen Orthodox synagogues and a Conservative synagogue for the German community. Altogether there are twenty synagogues in the country, but only six hold weekly Shabbat services. Kosher food is easily found, and there are several kosher restaurants.

Recently, however, many Jewish families have suffered from the poor economy, and the wealth of the community has declined. Many shops have closed from a lack of trade, and between 1998 and 2003, more than half of the community emigrated, most to Israel. Uruguay was the first Latin American country, and one of the first worldwide, to recognize the state of Israel.

Other Minorities

Following the conflicts in the Balkans, there has been a rise in the number of Muslim refugees seeking a home in Uruguay. The Muslim population is still small, and most have settled in Montevideo and the north of the country, close to Brazil. There is a Muslim center in Montevideo that announces the daily prayer times. Muslims face the direction of Mecca as they pray.

Approximately four thousand Uruguayans are Baha'i, or followers of the faith founded by the Persian Baha'Ullah. One of the youngest of the world's religions, it teaches that humanity is one single race and that the time has arrived for everyone in the world to unite.

Another small group are the animists. Mostly the descendents of African slaves, they retain a strong belief in spirits, or *orishas*, and practice their religion of Candomblé, or Umbanda. The followers have great faith in many aspects of the natural world, including herbal medicines and in the importance of certain days of the year. December 8 is devoted to pleasing the orisha Oxum, named after a river in Nigeria.

Among other powers, Oxum controls fertility. The faith is gaining momentum in many parts of the Americas and now has followers worldwide.

A priestess who practices Umbanda lights a candle to honor the African goddess of the sea, Lemanjá.

Culture, Arts, and Sports

U RUGUAYAN CULTURE HAS ITS ORIGINS MOSTLY IN European tradition. Unlike the culture of so many Latin American countries, it is barely influenced by the culture of the original Indian inhabitants. The gaucho, however, has been important in the art and folklore of Uruguay.

Opposite: **Dancers in Montevideo.**

Literature

In colonial Uruguay the two most important literary figures were Francisco Esteban Acuña de Figueroa (1791–1862), who wrote the lyrics for the national anthem, and Bartolomé Hidalgo. Although not a gaucho himself, Hidalgo (1788–1822) was one of the first poets to introduce gaucho and rural folklore into his writings. Juan Zorrilla de San Martín (1855–1931), known as "the poet of the fatherland," is regarded as the founder of modern literature in Uruguay. His best-known works are *La leyenda patria* and the epic poem *Tabaré*. Written in 1888, *Tabaré* describes the clash between the Spanish settlers and the Charrúas that ended in the destruction of the native peoples.

In addition to the novelist Juan Carlos Onetti (see sidebar on page 106), some important names in twentieth-century Uruguayan literature are José Enrique Rodó, Horacio Quiroga, Julio Herrera y Reissig, Juana de Ibarbourou, Mario Benedetti, Eduardo Galeano, and Mauricio Rosencof. Rodó (1872–1917) is considered by many to be Uruguay's most significant literary

The Gaucho Museum

The Gaucho Museum is in one of Montevideo's most beautiful houses, not far from the Plaza Independencia. The house is in the nineteenth-century French style with huge carved wooden doors, a highly decorated facade, and a marble entrance. A grand staircase of marble and polished wood leads to the first floor. At the top of the staircase are four glass cases containing life-size models of gauchos and their women in traditional dress (below). There is also a tableau of gauchos playing

the traditional game of *taba* and drinking yerba maté. In the first room on the first floor are five life-size models of horses with saddles and bridles used since 1830 (above). The remaining four rooms display gaucho equipment. One has whips and spurs in highly decorated silver, and another branding irons, lassos, bolas, and a variety of weapons including lances used in the war of independence. The third has facónes (knives), the gauchos' most valued possession. Next is a room full of belts and buckles, coins used as belt fasteners, and the precious tiny tinderboxes gauchos use for creating fires. The last room has a wonderful display of silver matés, the pots used for drinking yerba maté. In this room there are also large cow horns with silver tops that the gauchos use for carrying water. The museum is small, but its collection is superb.

figure. He achieved early acclaim through his work *Ariel*, published in 1900. In it he warned against materialism and technical progress in the United States and called on Latin Americans to find their own spirit. Herrera y Reissig (1875–1910) was the leader of a bohemian group of poets who challenged traditional forms of poetry, often using bizarre language. By contrast de Ibarbourou (1895–1979), one of South America's most famous women poets, used simple language to express themes of love and nature. Quiroga (1878–1937) wrote short stories, many of them about the struggle of man and beast to survive. He used the jungle, with its beauty and savagery, as the background for many of his tales. Benedetti (1920–) is concerned with urban life, and his novels por-

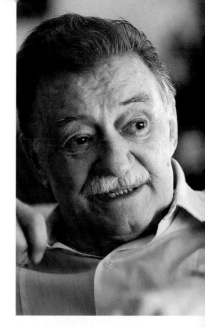

Best-selling author Mario Benedetti

Contemporary Uruguayan author Eduardo Galeano

traying Montevidean life are best sellers. Eduardo Galeano (1940–) was an exile in Spain during the 1970s. As a result of research he did there, he produced three volumes of a work called *Memory of Fire*, an unconventional history of North and South America. It established Galeano as a leading contemporary writer in Latin America, and he has since had many titles published. Rosencof (1933–) is a very popular playwright who in the past had been imprisoned on political grounds.

Afro-Uruguayan Literature

Afro-Uruguayans have made a significant contribution to the literary scene. The magazine

Nuestra raza ("Our Race"), founded by Maria Esperanza Barrios, was the longest-running black newspaper in Latin America. Major contributors included her brothers Pilar and Ventura.

Pilar Barrios (1889–1974) became a leading poet. His first book of poems, *Piel Negra* (*Black Skin*), was published in 1947. In it he called for liberty and equality for black people and denounced injustice and tyranny. Other volumes followed, including *Mis cantos* (*My Songs*) and *Campo afuera* (*Outside Country*), the latter devoted to the gaucho. Another Afro-Uruguayan writer was Virginia Brindis de Salas (1908–1958), the first black South American woman to publish a book of poems.

Art

Juan Manuel Blanes (1830–1901) was Uruguay's leading painter of the nineteenth century. His best-known works

Juan Carlos Onetti

Juan Carlos Onetti was born in Montevideo in 1909. Failing to complete his secondary education, he moved to Buenos Aires to work as a journalist. He began publishing short stories in the 1930s. *El pozo* (*The Pit*, 1939) was hailed by many as the first truly modern Spanish American novel. The main character leads an aimless life in a city, and this theme of a breakdown in urban life continues in many of Onetti's other books.

The three volumes of his Santa Maria sagas appeared in the 1950s. Santa Maria is a fictional city, but Onetti uses it as the setting for a number of his works. His principal characters are tormented people, and he writes with a mixture of comedy and sadness about the loneliness of life in the big city. His melancholy is reflected in some of his titles: *Tierra de nadie* (*No Man's Land*, 1941) and *Una tumba sin nombre* (*A Grave with No Name*, 1959). In 1962 he was awarded the Uruguayan National Literature prize, but his reputation failed to save him from imprisonment under the military regime in the 1970s. When he was freed, he left for Spain, became a Spanish citizen, and never returned to Uruguay. In 1980, the Spanish government awarded him the prestigious Cervantes literary prize. He died in 1994.

Juan Manuel Blanes' *The Battle of Rancagua*

Social gatherings were one of Pedro Figari's subjects for his paintings. This one is titled *Dance in the Courtyard*.

are detailed paintings of the history of the Río de la Plata region. At the turn of the twentieth century, Pedro Figari (1861–1938) was one of Uruguay's most prominent citizens. A successful lawyer, judge, intellectual, philosopher, founder of the *El diario* newspaper, politician, and finally vice president of the country, he didn't begin painting full time until 1921. His subjects included landscapes of the Río de la Plata region, social gatherings in colonial times, gauchos, and the folklore of the black

community. He chose soft colors and did not concentrate a great deal on detail; instead his paintings achieve a general impression of things. His work is internationally acclaimed, and he is recognized as one of Uruguay's foremost artists.

Another immensely multitalented artist of the same period was Rafael Perez Barradas (1890–1929). He was a draftsman, caricaturist, scenographer, illustrator, poster designer, and painter.

The person with the most impact on twentieth-century Uruguayan art was Joaquín Torres-García (1874–1949), even though he spent much of his life outside his native country. From the age of seventeen, he studied in Spain, where his early works included stained-glass windows and frescoes for churches in Barcelona and a series of murals. A few years in New York and Paris followed before he returned to Montevideo in 1934. There he created an art form known as constructivism. It is a form of abstract art made up of signs and symbols and created from a variety of materials, including wire, glass, and metal. In one of his best-known pieces, *Universal Art*, he uses shapes and symbols such as circles, squares, triangles, houses, boats, fish, and stars. One of his works,

The Cosmic Monument by Joaquín Torres-García

The Cosmic Monument, which is covered with many signs and symbols, stands in Rodó Park in Montevideo. Torres-García was a man of great presence, a writer and a teacher with many original ideas and theories. He had many followers, and in 1943 he established the Torres-García workshop in Montevideo. Some of his most outstanding pupils were Gonzalo Fonseca, Francisco Matto, and José Gurvich, and Torres-García's own sons Augusto and Horacio.

Carlos Páez Vilaró (1922–1995) is the Uruguayan artist who painted the mural that connects the two buildings of the Pan American Union in Washington, D.C. Completed in 1960, it is said to be the longest mural in the world. Other examples of Páez Vilaró's work can be seen in the extraordinary house he built near Punta del Este.

Casa Pueblo is the home to Uruguayan artist Carlos Páez Vilaró.

One well-known sculpture in Montevideo is *La Diligence* by José Belloni.

Sculpture

There are some fine sculptures in the parks and streets of Montevideo. Mostly they portray historic subjects from colonial times. Two of the best known are in Prado Park. One is *The Last of the Charrúas* by Prati. The other, *La Diligence*, is a full-size stagecoach and horses by Uruguay's best-known sculptor, José Belloni. Another work by Belloni is in the Batlle y Ordóñez Park. It is a life-size bronze statue of three yoke of oxen drawing a wagon, guided by a man on a horse. His last major piece of work is a statue of gauchos engaged in battle in Plaza del Entrevero.

Several works by sculptor José Luis Zorrilla de San Martín, son of the writer, can be seen in Montevideo. The best known, the imposing statue *El Gaucho*, stands downtown at the end of the principal shopping street, Avenida 18 de Julio.

The *El Gaucho* statue

Many folk dances center on the gaucho. In this photo children perform a traditional gaucho dance.

One of the oldest theaters built in Latin America, the Teatro Solís, holds opera and ballet performances.

European immigrants introduced their own music and dances, such as the polka and waltz, into Uruguay. The national dance is the rather stately *pericón*, for six or more couples. Folk songs and dances are often about the gaucho and his life on the pampas, and many have a melancholy air. Most are accompanied by the guitar or the *bandoneón*, an instrument similar to an accordion. Francisco Curt Lange (1903–1997), an eastern European who became a Uruguayan citizen, collected and published hundreds of the region's folk songs. Gauchos themselves like to take part in *payadas de contrapunto*, in which two singers compete with each other, making up verses as they go along. Early Uruguayan classical music had Spanish and Italian influences, but in the twentieth century a number of composers, including Eduardo Fabini and Vicente Ascone, have made use of Latin American idioms. The splendid Teatro Solís in Montevideo has hosted grand opera and ballet for more than 150 years.

Tango is generally more associated with Buenos Aires than with Montevideo, but it originated in the working-class neighborhoods of both cities in the late 1880s.

"La Cumparsita," perhaps the most famous of all tango songs, was composed by the Uruguayan Gerardo Matos Rodríguez in 1917, and some claim that Carlos Gardel, the most famous of tango singers, was born in Uruguay. Today Montevideo is bursting with tango. There are two all-tango radio stations, more than twenty tango dance halls, and seven tango schools.

Candombe and Carnival

African musical tradition has survived in the form of *candombe*. Candombe is played on three different-size *tambores*, or drums: the *tambor chico*, the *tambor piano*, and *tambo repique*. Groups regularly gather in the streets to play. A bonfire is lit to tone the hides of the drums, which when played together produce an incredible sound.

Candombe is a central part of Carnival, which takes place every year in February or March immediately before Ash Wednesday. Carnival has it origins in African traditions. The drums and rhythms are African, and the groups taking part have African names, such as Serenata Africana, Yambo, and Senegal, but in Uruguay, because the Afro community is so small, the many thousands of people who take part are mostly white. The central part of Carnival is *Las llamadas*, or The Calls. This is the

Members of a comparsas dance to the candombe during the llamadas parade in Montevideo.

parade in which more than thirty groups from Montevideo's suburbs take part. The groups, called *comparsas*, sometimes have up to fifty drummers. They progress through the streets in the Barrio Sur and Palermo suburbs while hundreds of followers dance and sing to the thundering rhythms. Everyone is dressed in brightly colored carnival costumes, and many wear large, garish masks.

Another feature of Carnival are the *murgas*. These are troupes of musicians, writers, and actors who perform on temporary open-air stages built around the city. Their shows, which combine song, drama, and comedy, are generally satires of the year's political and cultural events.

A Sporting Triumph

Soccer is the number-one game in Uruguay. As Eduardo Galeano wrote in his book *Football in Sun and Shadow*: "Every time the national team plays, no matter against whom, the country holds its breath. Politicians, singers, and street vendors shut their mouths, lovers suspend their kisses, and flies stop flying." Imagine, then, how it must have been in 1930 when Uruguay not only hosted but also won the first World Cup.

In those days the Uruguay teams were among the best in the world. They won Olympic gold medals in 1924 and 1928 before there was a World Cup. But they reserved their very best performance for 1950, when they won the

World Cup for a second time. Before an estimated 200,000 people, the largest football audience ever, Uruguay defeated Brazil in the Maracana Stadium in Rio de Janeiro, two goals to one (below).

Futbol (football), which is called soccer in North America, was introduced into Uruguay by British residents and crews of British warships at the end of the nineteenth century.

Uruguay soon became one of the world's leading football nations. Today its teams are not in quite the same league, but Uruguayans are still passionate about the game.

Uruguay has two professional football divisions made up of teams from around the country. The most successful teams are Peñarol and Nacional, both from Montevideo. So intense is their rivalry that after one

Futbol (soccer) is a popular sport in Uruguay. Children begin playing at a very early age.

match, nine players ended up in prison. All teams compete for the Copa Uruguaya, and the national team takes part in the Copa Américana and other international competitions. The most important matches are played in the main stadium, the Centenario in Montevideo, and are attended by huge crowds of enthusiastic spectators. Uruguayan footballers are also highly valued overseas, and every year about ninety join the best clubs in Europe, often for huge sums of money. Children start playing football almost before they can walk. Any spare piece of ground will do—the street, the park, the

Alfonso Cardoso of Uruguay carries the ball during the 2003 Rugby World Cup held in Chile in 2002.

beach—for a kick around, and there is never any shortage of volunteers for a game. Scouts are always on the lookout for young talent.

Other popular sports include baseball, polo, and rugby. Uruguay is one of only twenty countries represented in the Rugby World Cup. The country's long coastline and many rivers are ideal for sailing, yachting, rowing, waterskiing, surfing, diving, and fishing. For the less energetic, time on the beaches, horse riding, camping, walking, or having picnics along the seashore or the riverbank provide perfect relaxation.

There are also the thermal springs close to the Río Uruguay, where tourists and locals enjoy the steamy pools. Almost all the best museums are in Montevideo, and the city has many parks where families can play and relax surrounded by trees, lawns, and lakes.

Semana Criolla

Gaucho rodeos always draw a good, if noisy, crowd of spectators—and none more so than during the Semana Criolla (Creole Week), which takes places in the Prado neighborhood of Montevideo every year in March or April. The festival coincides with Easter Week, which in Uruguay is also known as Tourism Week. The Semana Criollo is very popular with tourists, particularly those from Argentina. The central attraction are the gauchos. In traditional dress they demonstrate their skills in horse breaking, stunt riding, and lasso handling. There are also exhibits of live cattle and sheep. It is a wonderful opportunity for families to take time off together and enjoy the huge asados of beef or sheep, listen to folk music, and sing and dance.

Daily Life

118

THE SOCIAL AND ECONOMIC REFORMS INTRODUCED BY President José Batlle y Ordóñez early in the twentieth century gave Uruguay one of the highest standards of living in South America for many years. The state provides for people who are unemployed or sick and for employees who are injured while at work. Women with low annual incomes may receive maternity benefits and child-care benefits. There are also pensions for the elderly. But the problem Uruguay has been facing for some time is finding money to pay for all these benefits. A welfare state is normally funded by taxes paid by workers and employers, but the serious decline in the economy has meant that these contributions have fallen. At the end of 2003, 16 percent of workers were unemployed. At present it is estimated that less than 10 percent of the population lives in poverty, but this number could increase if the government cannot find the funds it needs.

In recent years large numbers of Uruguayans have moved from the countryside to the towns. They want better schooling for their children and better medical care for their families. They are also looking for work. Opportunities in rural areas are very limited. Most people own houses with only small plots of land. Near Montevideo they produce fruit and vegetables for sale in the city, and some grow grapes for the wine industry. There is little modern machinery, and all the family members, including grandparents and children, get involved in working the land. There is not much profit, and it is difficult for people to improve their lives.

Unfortunately for some, life in Montevideo and other towns is not much better. Well-educated people qualify to become doctors, teachers, lawyers, or bankers, or to work in business. People with technical training often work for themselves as plumbers, carpenters, builders, or mechanics. But semiskilled workers arriving from the countryside often find themselves doing odd jobs, sweeping streets, or setting up stalls in the main streets to sell trinkets or snacks. In Montevideo some may be lucky enough to get work in one of the factories. The new arrivals also may not find the medical care and schools they'd hoped for, as Montevideo and other towns simply cannot cope with the increased number of people.

Housing

People in the countryside may have only small houses with few rooms and furniture, but they usually also have a small courtyard or patio where they can sit and relax. Pretty tropical flowers decorate the patio, there is space for the children to play, and often there is a good view across the grasslands. Cooking is done on an open wood fire or, if bottled gas can be obtained, on a stove. For water many families rely on wells and windmill-driven pumps. When they move to the towns, the contrast could hardly be greater. The shortage of housing has led to the creation of shantytowns. Homes are made from whatever materials are on hand—wood, cardboard, even flattened oil cans. Few of these homes have plumbing or

electricity, though in some places electricity is pirated from nearby lines.

In the towns most of the permanent houses are made from bricks or concrete blocks, and in Montevideo many middle-class and working-class people live in apartment complexes. In the residential suburbs affluent families have large houses, with landscaped gardens and swimming pools.

Above left: **A modest home in Colonia de Sacramento**

Above right: **Middle-class and working-class Uruguayans make their homes in high-rise apartments.**

Health

Uruguay is basically a healthy country. Major illnesses such as smallpox, yellow fever, and malaria are either under control or have disappeared altogether. An important factor is that more than 90 percent of the population has access to clean water. Also, most Uruguayans enjoy a good diet. Meat, dairy products, fruit, and vegetables are plentiful and fresh, and local authorities run food kitchens for people who need help. In the countryside

Holidays

New Year's Day	January 1
Epiphany	January 6
Las Llamada (Carnival)	February or March
Semana Criolla (Easter Week)	March or April
Landing of the Thirty-three patriots	April 19
Dia de los Trabajadores (Labor Day)	May 1
Battle of Las Piedras	May 18
Birth of General Artigas	June 19
Constitution Day	July 18
National Independence Day	August 25
Discovery of America	October 12
All Souls' Day	November 2
Blessing of the Waters	December 8
Christmas Day	December 25

The largest state-owned hospital is the Hospital Clinicas in Montevideo.

most families grow their own fruits and vegetables and keep a few pigs and chickens.

Most of the best hospitals and medical facilities are in Montevideo, though there are hospitals in some of the departments in the interior. But those living in rural communities often have access only to a medical center that can deal with minor ailments. Any serious problem may mean a lengthy journey to the nearest town or a long wait for emergency services.

Going to School

More than 98 percent of Uruguayans can read and write. This is one of the highest rates of literacy in Latin America. Education in Uruguay is free, and all children from the ages of

José Pedro Varela

Born in 1845, José Pedro Varela wanted to be a lawyer when he was a young man, but he was made to follow his father into business. His academic talents soon became obvious, and while still a teenager he was writing for magazines and publishing poems. By the age of twenty, he was fluent in three languages. In 1867, he traveled to Europe and then spent eight months in North America. He met many intellectuals and influential people and returned from his travels enthusiastic about public education in these countries. In the 1870s in Uruguay, few ordinary people received any education. Varela began campaigning. He gave lectures, wrote articles, formed the Society for the Friends of Education, and

founded the newspaper *La paz* in opposition to the government. His main proposal was that everyone should receive free primary education. This, he believed, was necessary if Uruguay was to become a democratic nation. Not everyone agreed, and particularly not the church, which thought the idea much too liberal, and university professors. Varela worked hard to get his message across, and despite opposition, the Law of Common Education was passed in 1877. Varela died just two years later, at the early age of thirty-four. His reforms meant that by the beginning of the twentieth century, Uruguay's educational system was far more advanced than those of most other Latin American countries.

six to fourteen are required by law to attend school. About 90 percent of children attend primary school, which begins at six years of age. There is a drop in attendance at the secondary level, but at more than 70 percent, it is still high compared with attendance levels for other Latin American countries. The first stage of the secondary level, starting at twelve years of age, lasts three years. From the age of fifteen, students can choose to concentrate on academic subjects or technical training. Academic studies include arts, sciences, law, medicine, architecture, and engineering. After three years the successful academic student leaves secondary school with a *bachillerato*, and those who follow a technical course are awarded a *bachillerato técnico*.

There are two public universities in Uruguay, the University of the Republic and the Catholic University, and a private university, together with some other institutions for higher education. Earning a university degree takes at least four years, with most taking five or six years. The University of the Republic has a distinguished medical school that draws students from many other South American countries.

Schools in rural areas are generally of a much lower academic standard than those in the towns. There are fewer teachers and a shortage of even basic equipment such as books, pens, and pencils. The schools in the towns, too, have problems. They are often seriously overcrowded and have to run classes in shifts, so that children of one age group attend in the morning and others attend in the afternoons or evenings. About the same number of boys as girls attend school, and most classes are mixed. It is the students from higher-income families who tend to complete their educations and get to attend a university. Children from poorer homes often have to stop school and go to work to help their families.

Newspapers and Television

Newsstands bring international news to Uruguayans.

With such a high literacy rate, it is not surprising that more than one hundred daily and weekly newspapers are published in Uruguay. Most are produced in Montevideo, but provincial towns also publish their own newspapers. The leading morning newspapers are *El País*, *La República*, and *La Mañana*, and *El Diario* and *Últimas Noticias* are evening newspapers. Some papers are associated with political parties, such as *El País*, which supports the National Party. Uruguay's first television station began broadcasting in 1956, and there are now more than twenty television channels. Popular viewing includes sports, films, and *novelas*, or soap operas, which are broadcast several times a week. The country's first radio station began in 1922; now there are more than one hundred stations. Both radio and TV can be received in most parts of the country.

La Taba

La taba is a traditional gaucho game. It is played with a piece of bone, the *taba*, taken from the knee of a cow. One side of the bone is smooth and is the "good" side. The other sides are knuckled or misshapen. The object of the game is to throw the bone so that it lands with the good side facing up. While one person throws his taba, the other players take bets on whether it will be a good throw. In 1827, the game was banned because it became too aggressive. Money changed hands, and lives were threatened to ensure that bets were won. Although the game remains illegal, it is still played in rural areas.

Food

Uruguayans are said to eat more meat than people of any other nation, including Argentina. Beef and lamb are cheap and prepared in many ways. Asados, or barbecues, are very popular. So are *pucheros*, which are soups made with beef, vegetables, bacon, beans, and sausages; *chivitos*, which are Uruguayan steak burgers; and *milanesa*, which is breaded, deep-fried steak. There are several kinds of sausages, and most dishes are eaten with a variety of vegetables and salads. The European influence on Uruguayan food and cooking has been important. Residents of Colonia Suiza have introduced a variety of hams and cheeses, while the Italians have been responsible for pizzas and pasta, crusty breads, and pastry bars.

A popular food in Uruguay is grilled meat.

Mealtimes in Uruguayan families are much the same as they are for families in Europe or the United States. Breakfast is usually a light meal, with bread, jam, coffee, or maté. Lunch has traditionally been a large meal, but as more people spend their days at work, many now have sandwiches or a snack. Uruguayans eat dinner late. Most times the meal will include soup, steak, salad or vegetables, wine, cheese, and fruit. They also enjoy eating out. Montevideo has many restaurants, which serve both local and

One of Montevideo's many restaurants

Milanesa Uruguaya

Ingredients

4 thinly cut beefsteaks (about 14 ounces [450 g])
Flour
2 eggs, beaten
1 cup bread crumbs

Preparation

Roll each steak in flour, then dip in the beaten eggs before rolling in bread crumbs. For best results, refrigerate the coated steaks for an hour. Deep fry them in hot oil or shortening. Eat warm immediately or cold in a sandwich with tomatoes and lettuce.

international food. Montevideo also has many markets that are filled daily with fresh food and produce from the surrounding districts.

The Port Market

Montevideo's Port Market has been functioning since 1868. Beneath the massive wrought-iron structure, noisy vendors used to sell fruits, vegetables, beef, and freshly caught fish. Then it was transformed into one of the most popular eating places in Montevideo. Today it is filled with dozens of restaurants and *parrilladas*. Parrilladas are similar to barbecues. Large grills placed at an angle above beds of glowing charcoal embers are covered with cuts of meat of every kind—not just beef, but mutton, veal, and chicken. Sides of ribs and the best fillets of steak roast gently alongside great spirals of sausages such as chorizos, *salchichas*, and *morcilla dulce*, a black sausage containing orange peel and walnuts. The Port Market opens at lunchtime and very quickly fills with a noisy throng of people, from senators to shoppers. On Saturdays it is even more fun, as artists and musicians entertain on the street outside.

Future

Uruguay is well respected among the other nations of Latin America for its democratic traditions and stable government. It is for this reason that Uruguay is often called on to host or

A Traditional Custom

In Uruguay, Argentina, and Paraguay, people everywhere drink yerba maté. The custom started with the native peoples, who believed that maté had magical and religious properties. Gauchos took up the habit, and it spread among the rural population. Yerba maté grows on trees related to holly. The leaves are dried and ground into a fine powder. Traditionally the powder was put into a vegetable gourd or a leather cup, but today it can be put into a mug or a glass. Water is then added, and the bitter tea is sipped through a metal or silver straw called a *bombilla*. Uruguayans today carry around a vacuum flask containing water, which they use to mix maté throughout the day. When gauchos sit down and relax at the end of a hard day, it is customary for them to pass the maté pot or bombilla from person to person.

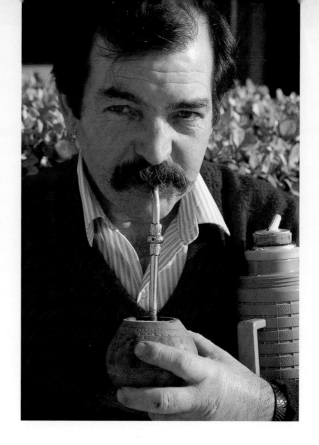

preside over important international talks, such as the General Agreement on Tariffs and Trade (GATT). The talks aim to reach some compromise on trade between the developed and developing nations of the world. Also, relative to the size of its population, Uruguay's military contribution to the United Nations Peacekeeping Mission is one of the highest in the world. Uruguay has also maintained its status as a leader in educational and social welfare reforms. For such a tiny nation, its contribution to sports and the arts has been remarkable. But there are difficult times ahead as the government tries to improve the nation's economic situation. Much will depend on Uruguay's neighbors, Argentina and Brazil, and whether they can resolve their own economic problems.

Timeline

Uruguayan History

Juan Díaz de Solís sails into the Río de la Plata estuary.	1516
Buenos Aires and Asuncíon, Paraguay, are founded by Pedro de Mendoza.	1536–37
Colonia del Sacramento is founded by the Portuguese on the north shore of Río de la Plata.	1680
Montevideo founded by the Spanish governor Bruno Mauricio de Zabala.	1726
Banda Oriental becomes part of the Viceroyalty of the United Provinces of the Río de la Plata.	1776
The British capture Montevideo.	1807
General José Gervasio Artigas defeats Spaniards in the Battle of Las Piedras; later that year he and thousands of other Orientales head into exile in Argentina.	1811
The Orientales fight for independence.	1812–20

World History

2500 B.C.	Egyptians build the Pyramids and the Sphinx in Giza.
563 B.C.	The Buddha is born in India.
A.D. 313	The Roman emperor Constantine recognizes Christianity.
610	The Prophet Muhammad begins preaching a new religion called Islam.
1054	The Eastern (Orthodox) and Western (Roman) Churches break apart.
1066	William the Conqueror defeats the English in the Battle of Hastings.
1095	Pope Urban II proclaims the First Crusade.
1215	King John seals the Magna Carta.
1300s	The Renaissance begins in Italy.
1347	The Black Death sweeps through Europe.
1453	Ottoman Turks capture Constantinople, conquering the Byzantine Empire.
1492	Columbus arrives in North America.
1500s	The Reformation leads to the birth of Protestantism.
1776	The Declaration of Independence is signed.
1789	The French Revolution begins.

Uruguayan History

Argentina gains independence.	1816
The Portuguese occupy Banda Oriental.	1821–25
The Immortal Thirty-three make a heroic journey from Argentina to Banda Oriental to resume fighting and defeat Portuguese.	1825
Banda Oriental becomes the República Oriental del Uruguay.	1828
General Fructuoso Rivera becomes Uruguay's first president.	1830
General Manuel Oribe becomes president but is deposed and succeeded by General Rivera.	1834–38
Civil war begins between the Colorados (Reds) and Blancos (Whites).	1838–52
Uruguay joins Argentina and Brazil in the War of the Triple Alliance against Paraguay.	1865–70
José Batlle y Ordóñez becomes president and establishes a welfare state.	1903–07; 1911–15
President replaced with nine-member council.	1951–66
Tupamaros wage guerrilla warfare.	1967–72
Military dictatorship governs the country.	1973–1985
Julio María Sanguinetti becomes president.	1985
Luis Alberto Lacalle Herrera becomes president.	1989
Julio María Sanguinetti elected president for a second term.	1994
Jorge Batlle Ibáñez elected president.	1999
Commission begins investigating the fate of people who disappeared during the years of military dictatorship.	2000
Tabaré Vásquez of the Broad Front is elected president.	2004

World History

1865	The American Civil War ends.
1914	World War I breaks out.
1917	The Bolshevik Revolution brings communism to Russia.
1929	Worldwide economic depression begins.
1939	World War II begins, following the German invasion of Poland.
1945	World War II ends.
1957	The Vietnam War starts.
1969	Humans land on the moon.
1975	The Vietnam War ends.
1979	Soviet Union invades Afghanistan.
1983	Drought and famine in Africa.
1989	The Berlin Wall is torn down, as communism crumbles in Eastern Europe.
1991	Soviet Union breaks into separate states.
1992	Bill Clinton is elected U.S. president.
2000	George W. Bush is elected U.S. president.
2001	Terrorists attack World Trade Towers, New York and the Pentagon, Washington, D.C.
2003	A coalition of forty-nine nations, headed by the United States and Great Britain, invade Iraq.

Fast Facts

Official name: República Oriental del Uruguay

Capital: Montevideo

Official language: Spanish

Montevideo

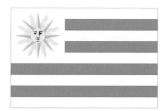

Uruguay's flag

Saint Teresa National Park

Official religion:	None
Year of founding:	1828
National anthem:	"Orientales, la patria o la tumba" ("Orientales, the Fatherland or Death")
Government:	Multiparty republic with two legislative houses—a Chamber of Senates and a Chamber of Representatives
Chief of state:	President
Area:	68,039 square miles (176,220 sq km)
Geographic coordinates:	33 00 S, 56 00 W
Land and water borders:	Brazil to the north and northwest, Argentina to the west and south, the Río de la Plata to the southwest, and Atlantic Ocean to the east
Highest elevation:	Cerro Catedral, 1,683 feet (513 m) above sea level
Lowest elevation:	Sea level along the coast
Average temperatures:	Montevideo, 61°F (16°C); Salto, 66°F (18°C)
Average annual rainfall:	Montevideo, 37.4 inches (95 cm); Salto, 50.3 inches (128 cm)
National population (2004 est.):	Almost 3.5 million

Population of largest cities (2004 est):

Montevideo	1,346,900
Salto	103,800
Paysandú	78,700
Las Piedras	73,000
Rivera	67,800

Seals on Isla de Lobos

Famous landmarks: ▶ *Catedral Matriz, Plaza de la Constitución, El Cabildo, Port Market, Teatro Solís*, Montevideo

▶ *Punta del Este and its beaches*

▶ *Sea lion colony*, Isla de Lobos

▶ *Casa Pueblo, house of artist Carlos Páez Vilaró*, Punta Ballena

▶ *Parque Nacional Santa Teresa* and *colonial fort of Santa Teresa*

▶ *Colonia del Sacramento*, a World Heritage site

▶ *Museum of the Liebig meat-extract factory*, Fray Bentos

▶ *Sand dunes*, Cabo Polonia

▶ *Thermal swimming pools*, Termas de Daymán

Industry: Agriculture is the basis of Uruguay's economy. More than three-quarters of the land is given over to rearing livestock. Cattle and sheep are raised for export as live animals and for their meat, wool, and hides. The main export crop is rice, but wheat, sugar, oil-seed crops, and citrus fruits are also grown for the export and domestic markets. Manufacturing industry is based on agricultural products. The most important products are processed foods and drinks. Vehicles are also assembled. Uruguay has few mineral resources. Construction materials such as sand, clay, limestone, and granite are the main mineral products, though semiprecious stones and some gold and silver are also mined.

Currency: The new peso is Uruguay's basic monetary unit. Exchange rate, 2004: US$1 to 26.30 New Pesos

Currency

Folkdancers

Weights and measures:	Metric system is in use	
Literacy:	98 percent (2003 est.)	

Common Spanish words and phrases:

adiós (ah-dee-OHS)	good-bye
buenos días (BWAHN-ohs DEE-yahs)	good morning
buenos noches (BWAHN-ohs NOH-ches)	good evening/ good night
cuánto? (KWAHN-toh)	how much?
cuantos? (KWAHN-tohs)	how many?
dónde esta? (DOHN-day ess-TAH)	where is?
gracias (GRAH-see-ash)	thank you
no (nah)	no
por favor (pohr fah-VOHR)	please
sí (see)	yes

Famous Uruguayans:

José Gervasio Artigas *Independence hero*	(1764–1850)
Juan Carlos Onetti *Writer*	(1909–1994)
José Batlle y Ordóñez *President and social reformer*	(1856–1929)
Joaquín Torres-García *Artist*	(1874–1949)
Obdulio Varela *Footballer*	(1917–1996)
Juan Zorrilla de San Martín *Poet*	(1855–1931)
José Pedro Varela *Education reformer*	(1845–1879)

José Gervasio Artigas

To Find Out More

Nonfiction

▶ Bao, Sandra; Ben Greensfelder; Carolyn Hubbard; Alan Murphy; Danny Palmer Lee. *Argentina, Uruguay and Paraguay*, 4th edition. Oakland, CA: Lonely Planet Publications, 2002.

▶ Haverstock, Nathan A. *Uruguay in Pictures* (Visual Geography Series). Minneapolis: Lerner Publications, 1999.

▶ Jermyn, Leslie. *Uruguay*. Tarrytown, NY: Benchmark Books, 1999.

▶ Shields, Charles. *Uruguay*. Broomall, PA: Mason Crest Publishers, 2003.

Web Sites

▶ **CIA World Factbook**
http://www.cia.gov/cia/publications/factbook/geos/uy.html
An excellent overview of the geography, government, and economy of Uruguay.

▶ Candombe

http://www.candombe.com/
english.html

Colorful site of the history of candombe and its arrival with black slaves from Africa; includes information on festivals and events and the instruments used, along with paintings by Pedro Figari and others.

Organizations and Embassies

▶ **Embassy of Uruguay**
2715 M St., NW, 3rd floor
Washington, DC 20007
(202) 331-1313

Index

Page numbers in *italics* indicate illustrations.

A

Acuña de Figueroa, Francisco Esteban, 103
Afro-Uruguayans, 85, 90, 105–106
agriculture. *see also gauchos* (cowboys)
    crops, 29, 43, 77–78, 79
    floods and, 24
    immigrants and, 55, 87
    livestock, 10, 47, 48, 75–77, 79, 89
    small farmers, 119–120
Alvarez, Gregorio, 60
amnesty, 61, 68–69
amphibians, 32
Anglican Church, 97
animals. *see* livestock; wildlife
animism, 100–101
Argentina
    border with, 23
    economy and, 73, 74, 127
    energy sources and, 21–22, 81
    independence of, 51
    relations with, 54, 58
Arias, Hernando, 47, 48
Ariel (Rodó), 105
Arroyo Guaviyú, 23
art and artists, 106–111
Artigas, José Gervasio, *52, 52,* 92
Ascension Island, 39
Ascone, Vicente, 112
Asunción, Paraguay, 47

Atlantic Ocean, 26
automobiles. *see* cars

B

Bahaism, 100
Banda Oriental, 28, 46–47
bandoneón (musical instrument), 112
banks, 74, 75
Barrios, Maria Esperanza, 106
Barrios, Pilar, 106
Batlle Ibáñez, Jorge, 65, *65–66,* 99
Batlle y Grau Lorenzo, 66
Batlle y Ordóñez, José, 10, 56–57, 66, *66,* 95, 119
Battle of Rancagua, The (Blanes), *107*
Belloni, José, 110
Benedetti, Mario, 103, *105,* 105
Bioshere Reserve of the Eastern Wetlands, 43
birds, 32, 33, 35, 36, 38
Blancos (political party), 53–54, 56–57, 59, 61
Blanes, Juan Manuel, 106–107
bolas, 45
Borda, Idiarte Juan, 56
Bordaberry, Juan María, 59, 60, *60*
Brazil, 17, 20, 27, 73, 74, 81, 127
bridges, 23
Brindis de Salas, Virginia, 106
Broad Front, the, 63–64

Buenos Aires, 47
butiá palms, 43

C

Cabot, Sebastian, 46, 47, *47*
cabybaras, 36, *36*
cachilas (cars), 9
Campo afuera (Barrios), 106
candombe (music), 113
Cardoso, Alfonso, *116*
Carnival, 113–114
cars, 9, 11, 12, 81
Casa Pueblo, *109*
Cascades of Queguay, 23
Castro, Fidel, 59
Catedral Matriz, 13, 70–71, 97, *97*
Catholic Church, 57, 95, 96
Catholic University, 123
Cenenario stadium, 115
Cerro Catedral, 18
Cerro de las Ánimas, 19
Charrúa people
    European settlement and, 45, 46,
        48, 86–87
    gauchos (cowboys) and, 92
    legends of, 19
    literature and, 103
    religion and, 95
Christianity, 96–98
Christmas, 96
cites, 28–29, 87. *see also* Montevideo
civil war, 53–54, 56, 66
climate, 27, 76
clothing, 93
coastline, 26–27, 83
Colonia del Sacremento, 28, 49,
    49–50, 83
Colonia El Ombú, 88
colonial Uruguay, 48–50

Colonia Suiza (town), 89, 125
Colorados (political party)
    Batlle y Ordóñez, José and, 56–57,
        66
    civil war and, 53–54
    elections and, 61, 63–64, 65–66
    post-World War II, 58–59
common markets, 73
Communist Party, 60, 63
Congress, 61, 65, 68, 69
conservation. *see* environmentalism
constitution, 67–69
Coro Pro-Musica de Treinta y
    Tres, 29
Cosmic Monument, The
    (Torres-García), *108*, 108–109
Council of Ministers, 67–68
Council of State, 59–60, 61, 63
coups, military, 12
courts, 68
cowboys. *see gauchos* (cowboys)
coypu, 36, 36–37
cricket (sport), 88
crops, 29, 43, 77–78, 79
Cuban Revolution, 59
Cuchilla de Haedo, 18, 21, 23
Cuchilla Grande, 18, 27
Cuchilla Negra, 21
cuchillas (hills), 17–18
currency, 74, 75
Cypella herberti (iris), 43

D

dairy industry, 89
dams, 21–22, 24, 25, 29
dance. *see* music and dance
Dance in the Courtyard (Figari), *107*
departments, of Uruguay, 68, 69
día, El (newspaper), 66

diario, El (newspaper), 107
Díaz de Solís, Juan, 46, 47
Diligence, La (Belloni), 110, *110*
drought, 76

E

Easter, 96
economy
    bank crisis, 74–75
    development of, 54–55
    future of, 127
    industry and, 11, 57
    political parties and, 58–59, 61
    reforms, 61, 63, 119
    weakness of, 66, 73
education, 57, 95–96, 99, 122–124
elections, 59, 60, 61, 67, 68, 69
Embalse Rincón de Bonete, 17, 24, 25
emigration, 89, 100
employment, 57, 66, 73, 75, 93,
    119–120
endangered species, 43
energy sources, 21–22, 29, 81
environmentalism, 33–35, 41, 41–43
estancias (ranches), 13, 86, 88, 93.
    see also gauchos (cowboys)
executive branch, 67–68, 69
explorers, European, 45, 46–47
exports. *see* trade

F

Fabini, Eduardo, 112
facónes (knives), 93, 104
Fast Facts, 130–133
festivals, 93
Figari, Pedro, 107–108
fish, 32, 41, 78, 79
flags, 63, *63*

flamingos, Chilean, *36*, 36
floods, 24
Flores, Venancio, 54
flowers, 34
folklore, 14, 19, 36, 38, 103
folk songs, 112
Fonseca, Gonzalo, 109
foods, 93, 99, 120–121, *121–122*, 125–126
foot-and-mouth disease, 74
Football in Sun and Shadow (Galeano), 114
forests, 31, 42–43, 78
Franciscana river dolphins, 41
Fray Bentos (town), 11, 23, 56

G

Galeano, Eduardo, 103, *105*, 105, 114
games, 124
Gardel, Carlos, 113
Gaucho, El (Zorrilla), 111, *111*
"Gaucho Martín Fierro, The" (Hernandez), 15
Gaucho Museum, 104
gauchos (cowboys), 13–15, *14*, *92*, 92–93, *93*
    Gaucho Museum, 104
    literature and, 103
    music of, 112
    origins of, 48, 86
    rodeos, 117
General Agreement on Tariffs and Trade (GATT), 127
General Artigas International Bridge, 23
geology, 17–19, 20
German Evangelist church, 87
government
    branches of, 67–69
    cars and, 9
    civil war, 12, 53–54, 56, 66
    international role of, 126–127

political parties, 60, 60–61, 63, 64–66, 90, 124
    welfare state, 10–11, 61, 63, 119
Graf Spee (ship), 58, *58*
grasslands, *13*, 13–15, 31–33
Great Britain, 51
Guaviyú, 23
guerrilla movement, 59
Guevara, Ché, 59
Gurvich, José, 109

H

health, 86, 121–122, 123
Hernandarias, 47, 48
Hernández, José, 15
Herrera y Reissig, Julio, 103, 105
Hidalgo, Bartolomé, 103
hills. *see* mountains and hills
holidays, 96, 121
hornero (bird), 36
hot springs, 21, *22*, 22–23, 116–117
housing, 45, 120–121
human rights, 60, 61, 95–96

I

Ibarbourou, Juana de, 103, 105
immigration, 10, 54–55, 85, 87–89, 98, 99
independence movement, 13, 50–52
industry, 55, 56, 57, 73, 79–83. *see also* agriculture; employment
inflation, 75
International Conference on the Conservation of Wetlands and Waterfowl, 34
International Union for the Conservation of Nature, 43
Internet, the, 97
Isla de Lobos, *33*, 40, *40*
Islam, 100

J

jineteada (festival), 93
Judaism, 98–100
judicial branch, 68, 69

L

labor laws, 57
Lacalle Herrera, Luis Alberto, 61, 63
Lagoa dos Patos, 27
lagoons, 26–27
Laguna Castillos, 34, 42
Laguna Merín, 17, 26–27, 34
Laguna Negra, 27, 34
lakes and rivers, 17, 19, 20–26
landscape, 17–19
Lange, Francisco Curt, 112
languages, 91
Last of the Charrúa, The (Prati), 86–87, 110
la taba (game), 124
Lavalleja, Juan Antonio, 28
legislative branch. *see* Congress
Legislative Palace, 67
leyenda patria, La (Zorrilla), 103
literature, 14–15, 103, 105–106
livestock, 47, 48, 74, 75–77, 79
llamadas, Las (Carnival parade), 113–114
Lobo, Manuel, 28
Lubakov, Vasilli, 98

M

magazines, 105–106
mammals, 36–37
maps
    European exploration, 46
    Montevideo, *71*
    native peoples, *45*
    natural resources, *76*
    population, 86

South America, *54*
    Uruguay, *15*, *18*, *49*, 68
Matos Rodriguez, Gerardo, 113
Matto, Francisco, 109
meat industry, 11, 56
Memory of Fire (Galeano), 105
Méndez, Aparicio, 60
Mendoza, Pedro de, 47
Mennonites, 88
Mercosur (Southern Cone Common Market), 73
mestizos, 85, 86
Milanesa Uruguaya (recipe), 126
military, 61, 66, 68–69, 127
military rule, 59–60
minerals. *see* rocks and minerals
mining, 80
Mirador Nacional, 19
Mis cantos (Barrios), 106
missionaries, 48, 86, 95, 97
Montevideo, 12–13, 17, *70*, 70–71, *71*
    development of, 55
    elections and, 64
    population of, 85, 87
    settlement of, 50, 51
Mormon Church, 97
mountains and hills, 17–19
Mundo Afro, 90
murgas (street performers), 114
Museum of the Industrial Revolution, 11–12
museums, 11–12, 104, 117
music and dance, 29, 67, 103, 112–114
Muslim people, 100

N

Napoléon, 51
national anthem, 67, 103
national monuments, 22

national parks, 26
National Party, 64, 66.
    see also Blancos
National System of Protected Rural Areas, 33
native peoples. *see* Charrúa people
natural resources, maps of, 76
New Israel, 98
newspapers, 51, 66, 107, 122, 124
Nuestra raza (magazine), 105–106
Nuevo Berlin, 87

O

ocelots, 33
Olympic Games, 114
ombú trees, 42–43
Onetti, Juan Carlos, 103, 106
Oribe, Manuel, 53, 54
otters, 37
Oxum (spirit), 100–101

P

Páez Vilaro, Carlos, 109
Palmar Constitución Dam, 25
Palmares of Guaviyú, 32
palm savannas, 32
pampas deer, *37*, 37
pampas grass, *31*, 31
parades, 113–114
Paraguay, 73
parrilladas (barbecue), 126
payadas de contrapunto (song), 112
Paysandú, 23
Paz, La (newspaper), 122
Pelotas River, 20
Perez Barradas, Rafael, 108
pericón (dance), 112
Perón, Juan, 58
Piel Negra (Barrios), 106

Pintura Constructiva (Torres-
García), 75
plants, 31, 43
Plaza de la Constitución, *12*, 12–13,
70–71
Plaza Matriz. *see* Plaza de la
Constitución
poetry, 14–15, 105, 106
political parties, 53–54, 60–61, 63,
64–65, 90, 124
political prisoners, 60, 65, 106
population, 85, 86, 87
Port Market, the, 126
ports, 82
Portugal, 48–50
"Portuñol", 91
pozo, El (Onetti), 106
presidency, 53, 59, 61, 67
Progressive Encounter coalition.
see Broad Front, the
Protestant churches, 97
Punta del Este, 83

Q

Quebrada de los Cuervos Reserve, 38
Queguay Chico, 23
Quiroga, Horacio, 103, 105

R

race, 85
radio stations, 124
railroads, 81
Ramsar sites, 34–35, 41–43
ranches. *see estancias* (ranches)
Rau, Johannes, 99
recreation, 83, 115–117, 124
referendums, 68–69

reforms, government, 10–11, 57, 66
religion, 48, 86, 87, 88, 95–101
restaurants, 125–126
rheas, *30*, 33
Rincón de los Gauchos, 23
Río Arapey Grande, 21
Río Cebolatti, 27, 35
Río Cuareim, 21
Río Daymán, 22
Río de la Plata, 12, 17, 19, *25*, 25–26,
32, 47
Río Negro, 19, 23, 24–25, *25*
Río Olimar Grande, 27, 34–35
Río Paraguay, 46
Río Paraná, 25, 26, 46
Río Queguay Grande, 23
Río Uruguay, 17, 19, 20–23, 26, 83
Río Yi, 25
Rivera, Fructuoso, 53–54
rivers. *see* lakes and rivers
rocks and minerals, 20, 80
Rodó, José Enrique, 103, 105
Rosas, Juan Manuel de, 54
Rosencof, Mauricio, 103, 105
rugby, 116
Russian Orthodox Church, 98

S

Salto, 29, *29*, 78
Salto Hydroelectric Dam, *21*, 21–22,
29, 81
sand dunes, 26
Sanguinetti, Julio Maríĺa, 60, *60*, 61,
64, 66
San Javier (town), 88–89, 98
San Salvador (town), 46
Santa Teresa National Park, 26, 41, *42*

schools. *see* education
sculpture, 110–111
sea lions, 40
seals, 33, 40
Semana Criolla, 117
Sendic, Raúl, 59, 60
Seriemas (bird), 38
settlement, 9–10, 23, 46–50
Seven Villages of the Missions of the Oriental, 95
shantytowns, 120–121
sheep. *see* livestock
shipwrecks, 26, 40
slavery, 90
snakes, 32
soccer, 114, 115–116
Socialist Party, 64
Soriano (town), 23
South America, map of, *54*
Southern Cone Common Market, 73
southern screamer (bird), 36
Southern Star, The (newspaper), 51
Spain, 9–10, 48–50
sports, 88, 114, 115–116
standard of living, 119
strikes, 61, 63
sunflowers, *77*
Supreme Court, 68
Suriname, 17
synagogues, 99

T

Tabaré (Zorrilla), 103
Tacuarembó, 18, 25
tamandua anteater, 38, *38*
tango, 112–113
taxes, 50

Teatro Solís, *112*, 112
television, 124
Termas de Arapey, 21
Termas de Daymán, 22
Termas de Guaviyú, *22*
textiles, 55
theatre, 105, 114
Thirty-Three, the, 52
Tierra de nadie (Onetti), 106
Timeline, 128–129
Toribio, Tomás, 97
Torres-García, Augusto, 109
Torres-García, Horacio, 109
Torres-García, Joaquín, 75, 108–109
tourism, 58, 74, 82–83, 92, 117
town hall, old, 13, 71
towns and villages, 13, 85, 88–89
trade
    colonial, 50
    energy sources and, 81
    General Agreement on Tariffs and Trade (GATT), 127
    immigrants and, 87
    international, 57, 58, 73, 74, 82
transportation, 55, 81–82. *see also* cars
trees. *see* forests
Treinta y Tres (town), 28–29
tumba sin nombre, Una (Onetti), 106
Tupamaros, 59, 64
turtles, 39, *39*

U

unemployment, 75, 119
unions, trade, 60, 61
United Nations, 28, 127
United Provinces of the Río de la Plata, 50

Universal Art (Torres-García), 108
University of the Republic, 123
Uruguay, maps of, *15*, *18*, 68
Uruguayan Bishops Conference, 96
Uruguayan National Literature Prize, 106

V

Varela, José Pedro, 122
Vásquez, Tabaré, 64, *64*, 65
vineyards, 78
Vizcaíno Island, 23
von Liebig, Justus, 11, 56
vultures, 38, *38*

W

War of the Triple Alliance, 54
water, drinking, 120, 121
waterfalls, 23
welfare state, 10–11, 61, 63, 119
wetlands, 31–32, *32*, 33–35, 43
wildlife, 32–33, 35–39, 41
World Cup soccer, 114
World Heritage sites, 28, 95
World War I, 11, 57
World War II, 11, 57, 58

Y

yerba maté (green tea), 93, 104, 127
Young (town), 88

Z

Zabala, Bruno Mauricio de, *13*, 13, 71
Zorrilla de San MartíIn, José Luis, 111
Zorrilla de San Martín, Juan, 103

Meet the Author

ARION MORRISON studied French and history at the University of Wales and soon after left for Bolivia to work among the Aymara people around Lake Titicaca, and the Quechua in other parts of the Andes. In Bolivia she met her husband-to-be, Tony, who was making a series of films about South America for the BBC. Together they have spent the past thirty-eight years traveling in Central America and South America, making television films, writing books, and creating a photographic library specializing in the region. They have two children, now grown up, who traveled with them many times in the jungles, mountains, and deserts.

"Uruguay is not a natural stopping place on the modern major routes through South America, so I feel fortunate to have stayed there on numerous occasions since the late 1960s," says Morrison. "The time span has given me the opportunity to see many changes in the country's fortunes, from relatively prosperous times through the days of the Tupumaro guerrillas to the present when the future is in the balance. My on the spot observations range from simple matters such as the

price of a meal in a fast-food restaurant to discussing the problems of wine exports with the marketing director of a vineyard. Uruguayans are very happy to talk about their lives and interests and here I must thank the dozens of ordinary people who have opened their hearts with information and family stories."

"In these days of Internet information I can call upon statistics and economics from Uruguayan sites in Spanish or from the United States and sources such as the World Bank in English. The cold facts can be put into perspective by asking people how far their weekly pay will stretch. But apart from these modern aspects of running a country I have always been fascinated by the history of the country wedged as it is between the giants of Brazil and Argentina. Uruguay may be off the beaten track, but I feel it offers plenty that is special including space and a gentler way of life."

Photo Credits